KU-263-025

Huntingdon

EIGHT CENTURIES of HISTORY

Huntingdon
EIGHT CENTURIES of HISTORY

Alan Akeroyd and Caroline Clifford

Published in association with

The **Hunts Post**

First published in Great Britain in 2004 by
The Breedon Books Publishing Company Limited
Breedon House, 3 The Parker Centre,
Derby, DE21 4SZ.

ISBN 1 85983 402 2

Printed and bound by Butler & Tanner,
Frome, Somerset, England.

Cover printing by Lawrence-Allen Colour Printers,
Weston-super-Mare, Somerset, England.

Contents

Introduction

THIS is the first detailed account of Huntingdon's history to appear for more than 25 years. This richly illustrated book has been written to coincide with the 800th anniversary of the granting of Huntingdon's first charter in 1205. For the first time, Huntingdon's modern history has been explored in depth, to accompany new research into earlier periods of the town's development. Covering a wide range of topics, ranging from priories to prisons, and from rationing to the ring road, this new book will make you view the town in a new light.

The publication of this book would not have been possible without the help of many individuals. We would like to thank Mrs Elizabeth Stazicker, County Archivist and Head of Heritage at Cambridgeshire County Council, for kindly allowing us to reproduce many images from the collections held at the County Record Office in Huntingdon. We also thank Chris Jakes of the Cambridgeshire Collection, for the use of images at Huntingdon Library; Paul Richardson of *The Hunts Post*, for the use of images and for the newspaper's assistance in publishing this book; and David Cozens, chairman of the Huntingdonshire Local History Society, for reading and commenting on the text, and for allowing us to publish items from his collection of photographs. Many of the images in this book are from the Whitney Collection of photographs, which comprises photographs taken by Arthur Maddison, Frederick Hinde and Ernest Whitney, and which are now held at the County Record Office in Huntingdon; we are grateful to Mrs Pat Collins of New Zealand for allowing us to reproduce photographs from this collection. The following people and institutions have also been a great help, by allowing us to reproduce photographs, or by commenting on the text: Bob Burn-Murdoch of the Norris Museum in St Ives; Alexa Cox of Huntingdon; Gilly Vose, Huntingdonshire Heritage Outreach Officer; Richard Young of Cambridgeshire Library Service; John Goldsmith of the Cromwell Museum, Huntingdon; Mrs B. Howes of Hartford; Miss Eileen Lewcock of Godmanchester; Professor Penny Sparke of Kingston University; Simmons Aerofilms Ltd; Martyn Smith, creator of the www.huntscycles.co.uk website; Martyn Webster of Huntingdon; Richard Kidd of Histon; the *Cambridge Evening News*; the Huntingdon Constituency Conservative Association; the *Peterborough Evening Telegraph*. We are also grateful to the staff of the County Record Office Huntingdon, especially Mary Croll, Jane Winter, and Jo March, for their assistance while we researched and wrote this book.

We have made every effort to track down the current copyright owners of all the photographs we have used. Any errors that may have occurred are inadvertent, and the authors welcome notification of corrections.

Finally, thank you to our families, for the patience and the encouragement they have shown. This book is for Nick, Helen and Andrew, and for Lesley; and, not least, for Andrew Akeroyd, whose arrival at Hinchingbrooke Hospital on 4 February 2003 has made the writing of this book such an adventure.

Caroline Clifford
Alan Akeroyd

CHAPTER 1

'Excelling all the neighbouring towns': Mediaeval Huntingdon

ON SUNDAY 7 August 1205 King John granted Huntingdon its first royal charter, confirming its rights as a borough and allowing it to hold a weekly market. It had long been customary for the Angevin kings to raise cash by granting royal charters to towns, and King John was in dire need of money following the extravagances of his brother King Richard, known as the Lionheart. Richard's foreign wars had taken a heavy toll on the coffers of England. Many English towns desired a charter during this period, as merchants in these urban areas wanted the freedom to trade, and they could easily afford the 'tallages' which the Crown imposed on their profits from time to time. Charters had already been granted in 1205 to Andover and to Ayr, to Hythe, Dover, Hastings, Sandwich, and New Romney: Waterford in Ireland had received its charter in July; Lynn in Norfolk was due to receive one in September. Many more would follow in the next few years. But 7 August 1205 was the turn of Huntingdon, a well-off town situated where the main road from London to Berwick crossed the River Ouse.

The borough charter granted by King John in 1205. Originally the royal seal would have been attached to the bottom of the charter. (County Record Office Huntingdon: Huntingdon Borough Charter no.1)

It seems that the charter of 1205 did not confer any new rights upon the town, but instead confirmed the rights its townspeople already believed they had. An entry in the *Anglo-Saxon Chronicle* for the year 963, which mentions the King's wish that there would be no market other than Peterborough's between Stamford and Huntingdon, is indirect evidence that Huntingdon already had a market by that early date.

King John had undoubtedly heard of Huntingdon, if only because the defenders of its castle had tried to kill his father. In July 1174, when John was just six years old, William the Lion of Scotland had inherited the title of Earl of Huntingdon, and started his attempt to dethrone Henry II. William's Scottish army took over Huntingdon's old wooden castle and fortified it. King Henry himself broke off his penance at the tomb of Thomas Becket to visit his forces besieging Huntingdon castle. The rebels surrendered on 21 July 1174, the King's success being attributed to his penance. The castle itself was razed to the ground and never rebuilt, although the site was fortified again during the Civil War. To judge from the layer of ash three feet thick uncovered by archaeologists at the castle site, the King's revenge on it was complete.

'Excelling all the neighbouring towns…'

Huntingdon in 1205 was an attractive place to live. The 12th-century historian Henry of Huntingdon, archdeacon there during the 1140s, described his home town as 'excelling all the neighbouring towns both in pleasantness of situation, beauty of buildings, nearness to the fens, and containing plenty of game and fish.' Huntingdon was wealthy enough to attract six monastic institutions (more than the rest of Huntingdonshire put together) which, as a 19th-century historian later commented, 'is a demonstration of the general goodness of the place: for the Monks always seated themselves in the fattest country.' The town was also a centre of literary excellence: Gregory of Huntingdon, who died in 1280, was a noted linguist, while Henry of Huntingdon himself was a gifted poet as well as historian.

The site of the castle. It was a Norman motte and bailey design, with the keep on top of the hill where the trees now stand. The modern A14 bypass cuts across the bailey, or courtyard, following the route of a 19th-century railway. (The authors)

Huntingdon in 1205 would have looked very different from today's town. Eight hundred years ago the surrounding countryside was deeply forested. Much of the Midlands woodland had been cleared by the Saxons, but a large expanse of wood still survived around Huntingdon; and the loss of so much woodland elsewhere only increased the value of Huntingdon's own trees. Reminders of this mediaeval woodland survive in local place names today, such as Upwood, Woodhurst and Woodwalton. The area to the east of Huntingdon was even called *Hurstingstone*, or 'People of the Wood'. Woodland was an irreplaceable source of fuel, timber, pasture, and fencing. Much of Huntingdon's woodland, however, was Royal Forest, which meant that it was subject to tight Crown control, and hunting was reserved for the King and members of his court. Ordinary people would not have been able to take advantage of the rich opportunities for hunting foxes and wild boar, chasing deer, or grazing animals.

After the castle was destroyed, mills were erected on the hill, as can be seen in this sketch published in 1818. (County Record Office Huntingdon: MC1/10)

The town itself had just one street, the High Street. The original Roman road which ran through the town was slightly to the west of the current High Street, but it had been realigned when the castle was built in 1068. At the same time the place where the bridge crossed the river was also relocated. Huntingdon's entire population of about two thousand people was clustered into tenements arranged higgledy-piggledy along both sides of the road. Most of the houses themselves were small timber-framed structures with thatched roofs. Behind them, there were allotments and small fields. There were also a few larger buildings: one such mediaeval hall was discovered at 45 High Street in 1975, but was demolished to make way for modern shops soon afterwards. The only stone structures were the churches. They had no pews, and their walls were covered inside with vivid paintings of Hell and the Last Judgement.

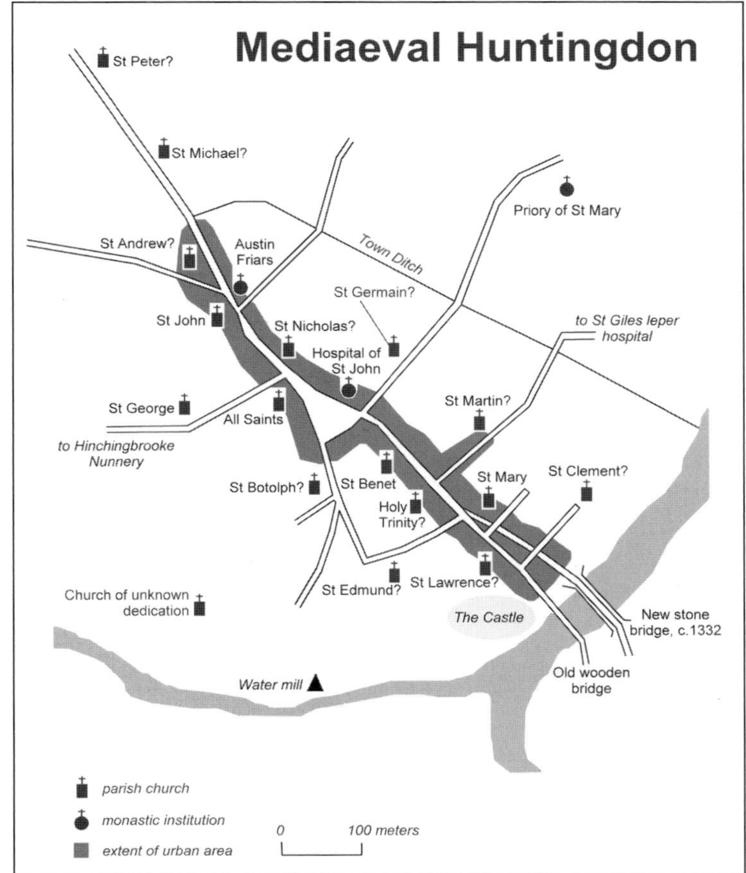

Map of mediaeval Huntingdon, showing where the churches are believed to have been located. (The authors)

The town's focus was its market square. On market days Huntingdon would be bustling with merchants and traders, while visiting friars preached from the cross which used to stand in the square, shouting at the townspeople and denouncing sinners. The town had several inns where traders and merchants would have stayed overnight. The shops themselves would have been below ground level, down a flight of steps, while the owners lived on the floor above. Both the square and the High Street were unpaved, muddy and awash with rubbish and excrement

Market Hill. There has been a market here since mediaeval times. (Huntingdon Library)

from animals and people. The only real attempt at sanitation for the town – the Town Ditch or King's Ditch, which ran along the eastern side of the borough towards the river – would have been a stagnant open drain, filled with waste and slime, and blocked with the rotting corpses of animals thrown there by the townspeople. Mortality levels in the borough, as in all mediaeval towns, were high, due to disease and injury. However, the town still attracted migration from rural areas.

The Town Ditch or King's Ditch, known more recently as Toby's Trunk. Early in the 19th century a well-known local mail coach driver called Job Rout, nicknamed Toby, used part of the brook between Spring Common and Great Northern Street to store boxes or 'trunks' of eels. He caught the eels in the meres around Ramsey, and kept them fresh in the brook until they were sold. (The authors)

Migration was the only reason why *any* urban area kept going during the Middle Ages. There was always a steady influx of peasants from surrounding villages, willing to sacrifice a secure but feudal lifestyle working on a manor, preferring instead to risk death by disease in the hope of making money in the town.

To get the most out of town life one would have to be a member of the town's elite, a freeman or 'burgess', which allowed traders to buy and sell freely, and to make profits.

Becoming a burgess was actually quite straightforward. A candidate had to be male, aged 21 or over, and the son of another burgess, in order to become one. Alternatively the candidate could simply move into the town and buy his burgess status: it was expensive, but simple. The burgesses of the town could freely sell or lease property without having to gain the consent of a manorial court, and they could vote or stand in elections for borough councillors.

People in mediaeval England moved around much more than one might think. This social movement is indicated by the derivation of people's surnames. Surnames were still fluid during the 14th century, and it was common for newcomers to towns and villages to be named after the place they had come from: 'John de Waresley', 'William de Hemingford' and so on. The lay subsidy taxation lists of 1327 show that only about 10 percent of people living in a typical village had 'de' names: five such individuals in Alconbury Weston, for instance, out of a total of 48 taxpayers, or five again out of 46 in Brampton. Huntingdon, however, had 25 newcomers out of 86, about 30 percent. Population turnover in Huntingdon, as in other mediaeval English towns, was high. This is one of the reasons why the rules allowing an outsider to become a freeman of the town were kept so simple.

People moved to towns to make money, so they tended to be traders, or individuals with skills such as leatherworking or metalworking. The earliest surviving will of an inhabitant of Huntingdon is for one such trader. William Scott the Elder drew up his will on 'the Thursday next after the feast of St Luke the Evangelist' (19 October) in 1340. He asked for his body to be buried in front of the crucifix in All Saints Church. More interestingly he bequeathed two *shope* next to All Saints churchyard to his son John, and another *shopa* in the parish of St Mary to his son

The wall of the 'Nunnery' at Hinchingbrooke. The Benedictine Nunnery of St James-Outside-Huntingdon was established at Eltisley in Cambridgeshire, but moved to Hinchingbrooke sometime during the 12th century. This wall, part of the kitchen range at Hinchingbrooke, is sometimes said to have been part of the Nunnery itself, but it probably dates from the 1550s. (Huntingdon Library)

William, both to inherit following the death of their mother Beatrice. *Shopa* is Latin for either 'shop' or 'workshop'.

Huntingdon's inhabitants would have practised many different trades. Some of those trades are mentioned in other contexts. In 1425 the Nunnery at Hinchingbrooke was violently broken into, and members of its staff were assaulted. The Prioress's account of the crime mentions the occupations of some of the townsmen who committed this outrage: they include a fisher, a barber, a smith, two glovers, a skinner, a cordwainer (leather worker or shoemaker), a hosier, and a chandler (candle maker). Yet Huntingdon was still dependent on the food and goods created by people living in the surrounding countryside. Many of the people who lived in Huntingdon would have needed agricultural skills to help support them, which was why the inhabitants of Huntingdon passionately guarded their rights over their common pastures such as the Great Common (split into Mill Common and Views Common by the railway in 1850) and Horse Common (today's Spring Common), which surrounded the mediaeval town.

Decline and fall?

In earlier years the thriving mediaeval town of Huntingdon had been even richer. The first mention of the town is in the *Anglo-Saxon Chronicle*, which refers to it as a 'porte' or market town. King Edward the Elder, son of Alfred the Great, had made Huntingdon the centre of an administrative county in 917 while the Danes were being driven out of England. A mint was created so that Huntingdon could issue its own money. There is archaeological evidence that the Saxons may have built a minster in Huntingdon as well. By the time of the Domesday Book in 1086 there were three 'moneyers' in Huntingdon, as well as 256 burgesses, 100 smallholders, and many others. These figures suggest that Huntingdon had a population of about 2,000 people in 1086.

Royal Oak Passage. This is the only surviving mediaeval alley in Huntingdon. Before the construction of the ring road there were many such passages leading off the High Street. (County Record Office Huntingdon: PH48/47)

These had been the good years. Since the 12th century, however, Huntingdon had been slipping behind in the economic race. Challenges to its prosperity came from many directions. The town's dependence upon river trade was threatened by all the new diversions, mill ponds, sluices, and dams which had been erected further upstream by rich families and monasteries, Ramsey Abbey in particular. From

1110 there was direct competition from the Abbey's new fair at St Ives which attracted international luxury traders in cloth and spices. In 1252 Henry III allowed Huntingdon to exact its own tolls on all river crossings while the St Ives fair was being held, so the town did at least claw back some money – in 1260, for instance, Huntingdon made almost £100 in this way. But the outbreak of the Hundred Years War in Europe meant that foreign traders stayed away, the importance of the St Ives fair waned, and Huntingdon's income fell.

A thriving town needs to be able to grow, but Huntingdon could not easily do so: town expansion was blocked on three sides, by the various commons and by the river itself. The only direction it could freely spread would have been towards the east, but there were royal forests in this area, and any expansion here would have taken it further away from the line of the Great North Road. St Ives had a more advantageous layout: its main street ran parallel to the river, making the unloading of boats much easier. But Huntingdon's High Street ran *away* from the river.

Mediaeval Huntingdon had other competitors besides St Ives: there were St Neots and Godmanchester to the south, and Ramsey to the north. St Neots, St Ives and Godmanchester all had their own markets by 1200. Between 1200 and 1250 the towns of Kimbolton, Ramsey and Caxton (in Cambridgeshire) received market charters; and between 1250 and 1400 further royal grants of markets were awarded to Earith, Fenstanton, Leighton Bromswold, Buckworth, Alconbury and Spaldwick. Not all of these markets succeeded, but they indicate the new culture of competition. Henry Bracton, writing during the 13th century, calculated that the natural catchment area of a market town was determined by the distance traders were prepared to walk, there and back, in a day. Bracton calculated this to be about seven miles. This meant that Huntingdon's market catchment area overlapped with those of many other markets, and so traders had a rich choice of markets to attend.

One way to react to these new pressures was to pick on an innocent section of the community and turn it into a scapegoat. In 1280 all Jews were ordered to pay a toll every time they crossed Huntingdon's bridge (until then they had been exempt if they lived in the county), and there is some evidence to suggest that Huntingdon's synagogue was burned down in 1287. But the persecution of part of the community inevitably had no effect, and Huntingdon's long-term decline continued. Huntingdon's economic problems were due to the success of its neighbouring towns, not to the activities of the town's Jews.

The population was declining too. As the town slowed down economically, it became a less attractive place to live. The Black Death, which struck Huntingdon in 1348, was the *coup de grace* which almost finished off the whole town. The Prior of St Mary and the Prioress of Hinchingbrooke Nunnery both died that year. In 1363 the new royal charter referred to this massive decline in fortunes of the borough, and stated that 'the town of Huntingdon, as well as by mortal pestilences thereunto coming, is so impoverished and injured that the fourth part of the town is not inhabited, and the remaining few have scarcely the wherewithal to live.'

Admittedly lots of English towns were failing by this time, and it is important not to exaggerate Huntingdon's problems. After all, Richard II borrowed £40 from Huntingdon in 1397, hardly a negligible sum; and the town managed to attract some immigration from the Continent, including a goldsmith, in 1436. Nevertheless the decline was real enough. From a peak of 256 burgesses in 1086 the number had dropped to only 54 by 1522. In 1461 life was so bad in Huntingdon that many of the burgesses simply abandoned the town when the Lancastrian army arrived on its progress south, rather than defend it.

Henry III's royal charter of 1252, which granted Huntingdon the right to hold an annual fair lasting for 10 days, beginning on the Monday before Ascension Day. (County Record Office Huntingdon: Huntingdon Borough Charter No.2)

Following the granting of its first charter in 1205 Huntingdon received a further 16 charters before 1630. Most of these confirmed and consolidated the town's existing rights, but occasionally new rights were granted. The 1349 royal charter, for instance, allowed the burgesses to build a prison. The main aim of the 1363 charter was to allow the burgesses to confiscate stolen property: a power they made the most of during the 1381 agricultural revolts, as the uprising was particularly serious in Huntingdonshire. The burgesses soon had so much power that a separate class-within-a-class emerged, the bailiffs, who did all the real work, making sure the market's regulations were being followed, checking the weights and measures being used, and punishing offenders. This informal hierarchy was officially recognised in the twelfth charter, granted by Richard III in 1484, which decreed that from now on Huntingdon's bailiffs and burgesses should form one legal body, the 'corporation'.

Saints and sinners

Despite the increasing power of the burgesses, the most powerful institution in mediaeval Huntingdon was the Church. Not only did it rule the townspeople's daily lives, and direct their beliefs, but it also owned most of the land, employed the most people, and spent the most money. The pre-Reformation Church commissioned nearly all the art that was created, and had a virtual monopoly on the education of children. Yet nearly all of the surviving documents refer to how *poor* the various Church bodies in Huntingdon were, rather than how rich. For example Hinchingbrooke Priory, a Benedictine nunnery which had moved to the outskirts of Huntingdon during the 12th century, was *always* poor. During the 13th century the Nunnery had to take in paying guests to keep itself going. In 1425 men 'arrayed in

Nun's Bridge. This crosses Alconbury Brook by the precinct wall at Hinchingbrooke. The original mediaeval bridge was built in stone, but much of it was rebuilt in brick when it was repaired and widened during the Georgian period. (The authors)

manner of war' had broken into the Nunnery, assaulted two of the servants and had made off with the cattle. By 1536 there were only three nuns and the Prioress herself left. Another monastic institution, the House of Austin Friars, set up in 1286 on Huntingdon's High Street, was also very poor when it was suppressed in 1538. The leper refuge of St Margaret's Hospital was so poor by 1327 that it had to turn away a leper sent by the King himself. Another leper hospital situated just outside the town in Hartford meadows, the 13th-century foundation of St Giles-without-Huntingdon, disappears from the records after the Black Death in 1348.

This poverty affected the town's churches, too. Sixteen churches are known to have existed at some time or another during the Middle Ages. We know the names of some of them from modern roads – St George, St Germain, St Peter – and the names of others from mediaeval documents. Two deeds for the Hospital of St John (now the Cromwell Museum) dating from 1265 and 1315, mention property in the parish of St Lawrence, for example. By the 1530s however, when English antiquarian and topographer John Leland noted the number of surviving churches, there were just four.

Some of these churches may have been established by wealthy patrons and subsequently foundered without their support. Some, too, may have existed only as small wooden structures, rather than the stone buildings we associate today with the mediaeval

St John's churchyard gates. St John's parish church used to stand on the High Street, but its churchyard walls are all that remains. John Speed's map of 1610 shows it had a chancel and a nave, but no tower. It was demolished during the 17th century. (The authors)

The stone bridge between Huntingdon and Godmanchester was built in 1332, replacing a timber bridge which was washed away by flood-waters during the winter of 1293–4. There was once a chapel on the bridge, similar to the one at St Ives. (Gilly Vose)

Church. The Black Death was a fatal blow to these smaller congregations and to their priests. At least 60 priests died or left the town during the Black Death, leaving churches without leaders. In 1348 there had been only 15 vacancies for new priests in the town, but in 1349, after the Black Death, this number had risen to 79. The parish churches of Holy Trinity and St Clement's both disappear from the records at this time. Holy Trinity was finally demolished in 1364, but even before the Black Death, Huntingdon's churches had been having a tough time. St Edmund's lost viability as a separate parish in 1313 and had to be united with St Mary's; St Martin's suffered the same fate in 1343.

The biggest single Church institution in the town at that time was the Priory of St Mary. During the 1200s it owned nine of the town's 16 churches, was responsible for the repair of the bridge, and operated the water mill. Over the centuries these activities brought the Priory into conflict with Huntingdon's townspeople. The mill hindered the flow of the river, making river traffic slow and difficult; while the bridge itself was continually in a ruined state. The Priory had helped to pay for a new stone bridge in about 1332, to replace the timber one which had been destroyed in the flood of 1293, but within a generation this new bridge was falling to pieces too. It was reported as being in disrepair in 1363, 1425, 1443, and twice again during the 16th century. The Priory was also responsible for seven other small bridges across the river, linking Hartford with Godmanchester: but in 1259 it was reported that the Priory was failing in its responsibilities to repair these as well. By the 15th century the Priory was frequently in debt. Unlike more fortunate monastic institutions like the Abbey of Ramsey, which was noted for its wealth, by 1532 the Priory in Huntingdon was 'as poor as Job'.

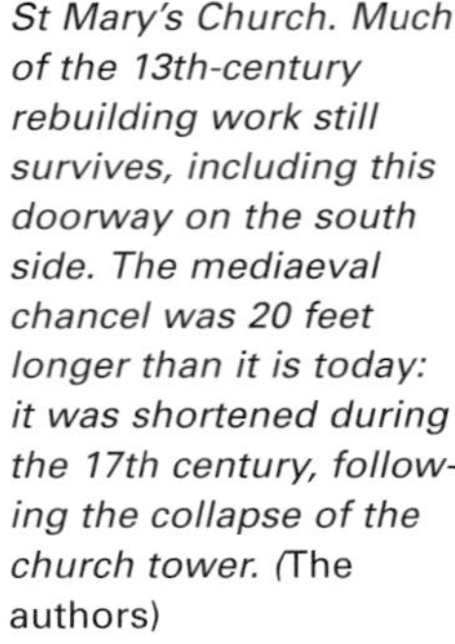

St Mary's Church. Much of the 13th-century rebuilding work still survives, including this doorway on the south side. The mediaeval chancel was 20 feet longer than it is today: it was shortened during the 17th century, following the collapse of the church tower. (The authors)

The Priory had also gained a reputation for corruption and immorality. In 1420 a scandal was caused by the revelation that the canons were having sex with the young women allowed into the buildings to do their laundry. Bishop Grey, who inspected the Priory in 1435, was concerned about the morality of the wife of a Mr John Clerk, living nearby: and his concerns turned out to be justified, as Bishop Alnwick's

The mediaeval stone bridge is not quite straight. This is probably because building began at both ends, and failed to meet up properly in the middle. (Gilly Vose)

inspection in 1440 revealed that she was one of Prior John Madingley's nine mistresses, and that another canon was behaving in a similar fashion.

All of Huntingdon's monastic establishments were shut down during the 1530s, with the sole exception of the Hospital of St John, which survived only because it was owned by the burgesses rather than by the Church itself. This foundation had been set up in about 1160 by David, Earl of Huntingdon and later King of Scotland, in order to provide bed and board for poor travellers passing through the town.

The Hospital of St John the Baptist, founded by the Earl of Huntingdon. Only this part of a much larger building remains: originally the Hospital included a great hall in Norman style, a chapel, and a two-storey gatehouse. Much of it was demolished in 1565. The western section, seen here, was converted into a school. (The authors)

By 1263 the burgesses had become the patrons of the hospital, and they controlled its finances and property. The hospital was formally wound up as a religious institution in 1547 but it was allowed to continue as a lay institution, and the burgesses eventually used the hospital's funds to set up the Grammar School in the same building.

Further damage to Huntingdon's ecclesiastical life during the Reformation was halted only because most of the town's churches had already failed. The Protestants tried to shut down many churches after the Reformation: Lincoln for instance lost more than half of its parish churches between the 1530s and the end of the 1550s. Huntingdon had *already* lost 12 of its 16 churches by 1530. There was simply nothing left for the Protestants to close down.

The old mediaeval world had gone. The major landowners in Huntingdon from now on would be private families, moving in from other parts of the country, suddenly rich from the dissolution of monasteries like Ramsey Abbey.

CHAPTER 2

'A Poor Decayed Town': Huntingdon under the Tudors and Stuarts

THE 1530s saw fundamental changes in English society, and the inhabitants of Huntingdon were affected just as much as anyone else. Following Henry VIII's break with Rome, religious belief and practice became the responsibility of the British monarch: priests and bishops now ultimately answered to the Crown. The most visible immediate change was the dissolution of the religious houses which had proliferated across England.

Because the monasteries had been a major source of urban revenue, their dissolution threatened the economy of many towns. The monks of the Priory of St Augustine and the nuns of Hinchingbrooke Priory vacated their buildings, moved in with friends and recusant supporters, and spent the rest of their lives living on the pensions granted to them by the Royal Commissioners. Their servants received no pensions and had to find new jobs. These were small institutions. Ramsey Abbey, however, was one of the wealthiest monasteries in England. Its wealth passed into the hands of secular families, bringing a new 'aristocracy' into the area. The Cromwell family was given most of the former Abbey's properties in Huntingdonshire, including the site of the Abbey itself, which they used as a summer residence. Most of the Abbey was pulled down and its stone was carted to Huntingdon and Cambridge, where it would be used to construct new buildings, including many Cambridge colleges, as well as Hinchingbrooke House where the Cromwells made their home.

All Saints Church, sketched in 1813. (County Record Office Huntingdon: MC1/2/16)

Those ecclesiastical buildings which were still used by Huntingdon's congregations fared little better. The chapel on the stone bridge to Godmanchester was converted into 'two little houses'. In 1607 the tower of St Mary's church collapsed, the event being recorded in the church's parish register: '*the Church of St Mary in Hunt fell down the eight day of July, being Wednesday between eleven and twelve o clocke in the fore noon, in AD 1607.*' The eastern and northern walls of the tower collapsed on to the rest of the building, smashing the north aisle and its adjoining arcades, and doing such damage that repairs were not finished until October 1620. All Saints church had deteriorated so badly by 1637 that a local rate was raised that year to pay for emergency repairs: the steeple was said to be ready to fall, the lead and stonework were coming to pieces, and a new communion table was needed. St John's Church, where Oliver Cromwell was baptised in 1599, decayed beyond any realistic repair during the Tudor and Stuart period, and it was finally demolished by Sylvester Bedell sometime between 1651 and 1660. Huntingdon was so poor that in 1663 the Diocese of Lincoln gave up trying to run the town's four parishes separately, and combined them, uniting St Mary's with St Benet's and All Saints with St John's. Huntingdon appears to have fallen into decline.

'A goodly prospect...'

One of Huntingdon's problems was that it was so small. On 10 May 1572 an unnamed Borough official walked around the entire town, recording as he went all the properties he came across, including all the houses, the shops, and the names of all the principal inhabitants. He started at the stone bridge, then worked his way up the western side of the High Street as far as Longmoor Baulk, the northern limit of the borough (where Spittals roundabout is today); he then walked back down the eastern side of the High Street to where he began. Even including short detours to itemise the properties on George Street and St Germain Street it came to just 281 entries. This same official then went on to itemise all the allotments, closes, fields and baulks around the town: but even these only added a further 143 entries.

Calculating the precise size of Huntingdon's population during this period is difficult, but modern research suggests a figure of about a thousand people, which was about half the size it had been during the 1200s. Historians sometimes use a figure of 4.25 as the average number of people living in a house: if we take the 1572 survey figure of 281 buildings then we arrive at a total of about 1,200 people. Calculations based on numbers of Protestants and Catholics in 1603 suggest a population of 745 inhabitants, and the 1664 hearth tax suggests it could have been as low as just 681 people: but later hearth taxes and other records consistently indicate about one thousand inhabitants. This means that Huntingdon would have been about the same size as many modern villages – Great Paxton and Great Gransden both have a population today of about 1,030 people, for example, while Hilton has 1,060 and Kimbolton 1,310.

A map of the town survives from 1610, drawn by John Speed, a noted cartographer who included maps of all the English counties in his book *The Theatre of the Empire of Great Britain*. The 1572 borough survey and modern archaeological evidence suggest that his map is wrong in some respects – Speed shows houses along both sides of Hartford Road, whereas they were really along St Germain Street, slightly further north – but in outline it seems an accurate representation of the town. Most of the churches and priories of the Middle Ages had gone: only the Grammar School and the four churches of St Benet's, St John's, St Mary's and All Saints now remained. To the west of the town lay a large bowling green, to the south a windmill, a water mill, and the gallows, where criminals were executed. In the Market Square itself Speed drew tiny depictions of a pillory and a market cross.

Huntingdon's houses would not have looked very different from how they had been during the mediaeval period. The High Street was still not paved, but it may have been cobbled. Inhabitants continued to get their water from wells dug under their cellars or in their allotments, and their waste would have been dumped into

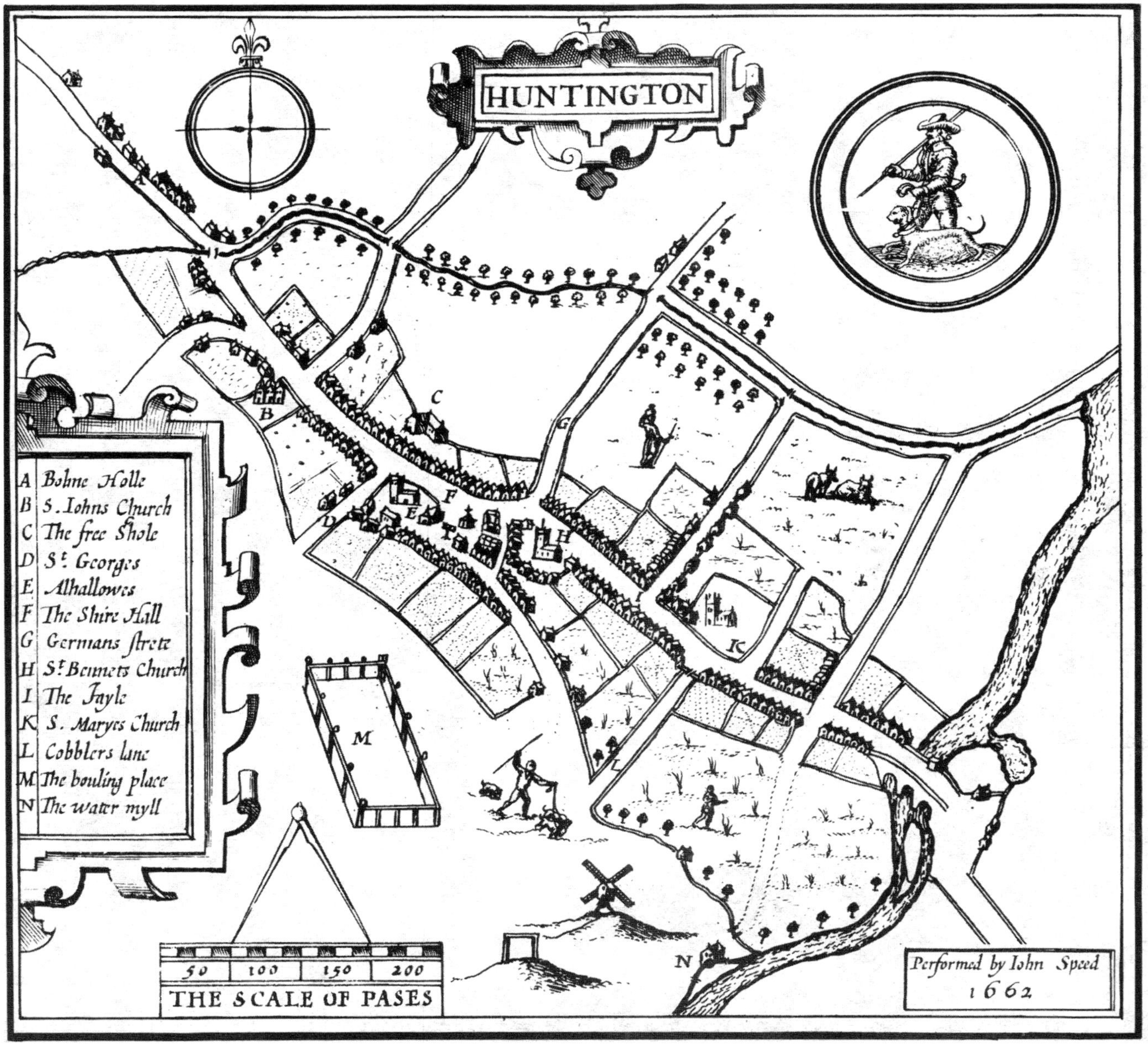

John Speed's map of Huntingdon, drawn in 1610. (Huntingdon Library)

the river or into the ditch running along the eastern boundary of the town. The houses were still single-storey timber structures with thatched roofs. Only a handful would have had a loft or second floor. The only major difference in the Market Square itself would have been in the shop fronts. Instead of being underground, traders had adopted the new style of displaying their goods on ground level, in their front rooms, while their families lived in the house behind. Customers could view the goods through unglazed windows. At night large wooden shutters were put up to shut the shop.

The mediaeval court house in the Market Square had been converted into a shop by 1572. A new court house was built during the 16th century, which included a schoolroom and wool chambers above ground floor shops. During the 1960s parts of a wooden house, dating from the mid-16th century, were discovered behind the façade of Cowper House, situated opposite the junction of the High Street and Hartford Road, which was at that time the main road to St Ives. This large timber building is described in the 1572 survey of the town as being the home of a bailiff. Other prosperous traders added extra rooms to their private houses, or refurbished them with glass windows and chimneys, even (if they could afford it) demolishing the old thatched timber houses to replace them with new brick-built, tiled-roof ones.

The Falcon Inn. Oliver Cromwell is believed to have addressed his troops from the first floor window. The building is largely timber, and dates from the late 16th century. (The authors)

The small mediaeval hostelries were enlarged, and new inns were founded to cater for wealthy merchants and travellers. Both the George Inn and the Falcon Inn existed during the 16th century, as they are mentioned in the 1572 borough survey. The George was already probably the town's most important inn, and was occupied by the Drewells, an old local family, while the Falcon was run by William Loungworth. It is possible that some of the present north wing of the George's courtyard may have been standing in 1572 when the survey was made.

Samuel Pepys mentions some of Huntingdon's other pubs in his diaries. On 20 July 1661 he went to the Crown in Huntingdon with a few friends, where 'we sat and drank ale and were very merry till 9 at night'; and on 17 May 1667 he had lunch at the Three Tuns.

Despite its small size Huntingdon was an attractive place to visit. William Camden was impressed with the town, as he recorded in his book *Britannia*, first published in 1588. 'From the Castle Hills, where there is a goodly prospect a great way off, a man may behold below a meadow which they call Portholme, environed round with the River Ouse, the same very exceeding large, and of all others that the sun ever shone upon most fresh and beautiful: whereof in the spring this may truly be said: *the pleasant spring fair flowers do yield, of diverse colours, in this field*. With such a delectable variety of gay colours it pleaseth and contenteth the eye.'

Hinchingbrooke House

The Cromwells arrived in Huntingdon in the late 1530s, having benefited from the Dissolution of the Monasteries. Sir Richard Cromwell alias Williams was a powerful figure in the Tudor royal court: his popularity with Henry VIII and his close relationship to Thomas Cromwell, architect of the Dissolution, resulted in him being rewarded with many grants of land in and around Huntingdon, including the estates of the former nunnery at Hinchingbrooke, the former abbeys of Ramsey and Sawtry, and the priories of Huntingdon and St Neots. Sir Richard's son Henry married well – Joan Warren was the only daughter of a wealthy London merchant, and brought with her a considerable dowry – and Henry was not averse to spending it following his father's death in 1544.

The Cromwells began work on converting Hinchingbrooke's buildings to a house for their family as soon as they gained possession in 1538. Many of the nunnery's

Hinchingbrooke House, as it appeared following rebuilding work completed in 1896. The West Wing, seen on the left of the photograph, comprised a set of servants' rooms built over an arcaded loggia ending in an octagonal tower. This wing was pulled down in 1947. (County Record Office Huntingdon: WH2/277)

The gatehouse at Hinchingbrooke. Architectural evidence suggests that this gatehouse was originally part of Ramsey Abbey; it was probably transported to Hinchingbrooke by Sir Henry Cromwell in the 1560s. (Huntingdon Library)

buildings were re-used, and the gatehouse was brought from Ramsey Abbey to create an imposing entrance. The new house was noted for providing every comfort and luxury available at the time, demonstrating the social importance of the family. Henry's lavish lifestyle so entertained Queen Elizabeth when she visited Hinchingbrooke in 1564 that she knighted him, and the freedom with which he distributed money as he travelled between Hinchingbrooke and Ramsey, allegedly throwing it out of the windows of his carriage, earned him the title of 'the Golden Knight'. He was Sheriff of Huntingdon four times, and represented the county at all the early parliaments of Elizabeth's reign.

Henry Cromwell was also fiercely patriotic, as he proved in 1588 during the crisis of the Spanish Armada. When news of the Spanish preparations reached London three armies were hastily put into the field to defeat the 30,000 Spanish troops, should they land: one on the southern coast, another at Tilbury to guard the approach to London, and the third held in reserve to be sent wherever required. Troops from Huntingdonshire were stationed with the Tilbury army. Sir Henry was Huntingdonshire's marshall, responsible for the training and equipping of the county's men and answering only to the Lord Lieutenant of the county, Lord St John of Bletsoe. On 17 June 1588 Sir Henry was at Greenwich, and issued orders to his officers back in Huntingdonshire to be ready to march with their men at an hour's warning, and that all the county's beacons should be put into a proper state, and continually watched. Sir Henry was head of the cavalry, and his eldest son Oliver was a captain of about 200 infantrymen.

The Cromwells were highly placed at court. Sir Henry and his son, later Sir Oliver, had entertained King James I lavishly at Hinchingbrooke on his journey southwards to London in April 1603. On 27 April 1603 Hinchingbrooke became one of the first households to welcome England's new king, James I. Huntingdon was well placed on the Great North Road, and a convenient distance from London.

It was surrounded by forest which could provide plenty of sport for the King, who was known for his love of hunting. During the visit, the Cromwells' hospitality extended to everyone in the Huntingdon area, rich and poor alike: it was noted that 'there was such plenty and variety of meats, such diversity of wines, and those not riff-raff, but ever the best of their kind, and the cellars open at any man's pleasure... as this bounty was held back to none within the house, so for such poor people as would not press in, there were open beer-houses erected wherein there was no want of bread and beef, for the comfort of the poorest creatures.'

This modern beacon on Castle Hill is a replica of an original 16th-century beacon. Beacons like this formed a national communication system in Tudor times. (The authors)

Unfortunately, James was so impressed by the hospitality he received from the Cromwells that Hinchingbrooke became a regular feature on the royal itinerary. This placed an enormous strain on the family's resources. Elizabeth I would never have imposed on one subject so regularly, but James was not so thoughtful. Feeding, accommodating and entertaining the royal party was enormously expensive, and, after the first few visits, Sir Oliver was not compensated with grants and offices from the King.

Possibly a portrait of Sir Henry Cromwell, popularly known as The Golden Knight, *painted by Adrian Key* (c.1544-c.1589)*. The portrait bears the caption 'Sir Oliver Cromwell' in the top left corner, but the style of painting and the costume of the sitter may suggest an earlier date than would be possible if Sir Oliver really had been the sitter.* (Cromwell Museum: HUTCM 117)

James literally treated the Hinchingbrooke estate as his own. No one was allowed to shoot or snare game in the surrounding forests. Scores of animals and wagons were requisitioned every time the court moved on. Accommodation had to be found for all the courtiers, servants and hangers-on who accompanied the King on journeys. James even left a store of clothes and other things at Hinchingbrooke. As early as 1605, he appointed a Keeper of the Wardrobe in the Manor of Hinchingbrooke for life. As a result of these depredations, as well as other financial setbacks, Sir Oliver was forced to sell Hinchingbrooke House in 1627.

A 19th-century sketch showing how Hinchingbrooke House may have looked during the 17th century. (Huntingdon Library)

Local people must have benefited from the regular visits of the royal court to Huntingdon. Merchants, innkeepers, and suppliers of meat, grain and other provisions would have seen an increase in trade, but overall the effect may have been more negative. Roads would have been churned up by the huge number of horses and wagons (more than 150 horses were requisitioned from Huntingdon and the surrounding area every time the court moved on). Farming would have been disrupted. Bedchambers would have been commandeered for the court's many guests and servants, which must have caused problems too. Worst of all, however, was that the court lost much of its mystique for the people of Huntingdon.

Hinchingbrooke House was bought in 1627 by Huntingdonshire's up and coming new family, the Montagus, originally a Northamptonshire family who had already purchased Kimbolton in 1606. Sir Sydney Montagu, who bought Hinchingbrooke, married Paulina Pepys, great aunt of Samuel Pepys. Their eldest son had been drowned in the moat at Barnwell Castle in Northamptonshire and it was partly because of this tragedy that they moved to Hinchingbrooke. Sir Sydney's son Edward was a successful Parliamentary commander during the Civil War, but became disillusioned with the Commonwealth and helped to negotiate the Restoration of Charles II in 1660. The King rewarded him with the titles of Earl of Sandwich, Viscount Hinchingbrooke and Baron Montagu of St Neots. Edward was killed in battle in 1672 when the English fleet was surprised by Dutch fireships in Sole Bay. His successors lived at Hinchingbrooke House for almost the next 350 years – they did not sell it until 1962.

Puritans and politics

Huntingdon's most famous resident, Oliver Cromwell, was born in the parish of St John on 25 April 1599, the son of Robert Cromwell, Sir Oliver's brother. The young Oliver attended the Grammar School in Huntingdon. The Grammar School had been set up in May 1565 by George Richardes, a London man, who made a

contract with the town's bailiffs that he would 'erecte, builde, fynish and make one suffycyent skolehouse' on the old Hospital of St John site. Richardes demolished most of the Hospital's buildings (which had probably become derelict and dangerous anyway, following the hospital's dissolution 18 years earlier), but kept one small part which he surrounded in Elizabethan red brick, hiding the 12th-century façade. Inside, he split the building into two storeys: the schoolmaster probably lived on the upper floor while the students were taught on the ground floor.

The schoolmaster during Oliver Cromwell's time there was Dr Thomas Beard, well known as an anti-Catholic preacher and author of the book *The Theatre of God's Judgements*, which first appeared in 1597. Oliver is traditionally supposed to have been introduced to the beliefs of Puritans in this way, but although Beard was anti-Catholic, there is no evidence to suggest that he was actually a Puritan. Many moderate Anglicans at that time disliked the papacy: and Beard, who served as one of Huntingdon's Justices of the Peace and who bought a prebend's stall in Lincoln Cathedral, was perhaps more moderate in his beliefs than subsequent tradition has claimed. Nevertheless Puritanism did flourish in Huntingdonshire. The whole region was a centre of Puritan zeal: even as early as the 1570s Bedford and Northampton were centres of evangelical Protestantism. There were at least two Puritans lecturing in Huntingdonshire during the early 1630s, Walter Welles at Godmanchester and Job Tookey in St Ives, so many people certainly had the opportunity to hear and adopt Puritan beliefs.

The Grammar School before the restoration of 1878. In Cromwell's time the exterior was surrounded by a red brick façade, but in 1878 this was removed to reveal the original 12th-century walls. (Norris Museum: PH/HUNTN/077)

During the late 1620s both Beard and Cromwell found themselves caught up in bitter town politics. Richard Fishbourne, a native of Huntingdon and a member of the Mercers

Cromwell House. Originally this was the site of a 13th-century Augustinian Friary, and it was still known as The Friars when Sir Henry Cromwell bought the property in 1568. Oliver Cromwell was born here in 1599. The house in which he was born had been demolished by 1724, and the present building dates from about 1810. During the 1950s this building was Huntingdon Research Centre. It is now a private hospital. (Norris Museum: PH/HUNTN/039)

Company of London, had died in 1625 leaving a large fortune. His bequest of £2,000 to the town created a number of problems, particularly regarding how the money would best be spent. Many burgesses believed that at least some of the cash should be set aside for a lectureship, and Beard (who after all was a lecturer) thought this was an excellent idea. Most of the other burgesses however, having been taught by Beard in the Grammar School and guessing what his lectures would be like, preferred to give the money to the poor. The arguments soon became personal. Officially the Borough Corporation was on Beard's side, as it would then be able to use the bequest money to pay for his lectures instead of paying him directly, but the Mercers Company disagreed. Even King Charles was drawn into the dispute at one point – he supported Beard. The Mercers appealed against the King's decision and their choice, Richard Procter, was appointed. That was not the end of the affair, however, as Procter was refused a license to preach. The matter was finally settled when Beard was bought off with a grant of £40. The dispute had taken six years. The first lecture was delivered in St Mary's Church in 1631. A few months later Thomas Beard died.

A pencil sketch of the Grammar School's interior, drawn by John Coles during the early 1840s. From 1565 until 1868 there were two floors: the schoolmaster lived on the upper floor, while the ground floor was a schoolroom. (Norris Museum: BMS/HUNTS/22)

The true significance of the Fishbourne crisis lay not in the personal rivalries it engendered but in its constitutional implications. The animosities stirred up by Fishbourne's will meant that Huntingdon's previously peaceful elections became riots. Some burgesses even decided that democratic elections should cease. In 1630, after five years of physical fighting at elections, King Charles I granted Huntingdon a new charter 'at the humble Petition of the Bailiffs and Burgesses of the Borough aforesaid, being willing, for the better governance of the said Borough, to prevent and remove all occasions of popular tumult and to reduce the elections and other things and public business of the said Borough into certainty and constant order.' The new charter replaced the old 'open' corporation with a 'close' one. Huntingdon would henceforth be governed by a mayor and a small clique of aldermen who would serve for life: and instead of being accountable to the townspeople, they would be accountable only to the Crown. Elections would not need to be held ever again.

This anti-democratic Charter would stay in force until 1835. All the richest men in the town were appointed aldermen under the new charter except Thomas Edwards, who had opposed the Borough over the Fishbourne lectureship, William Kilborne and Oliver Cromwell, who was merely appointed a Justice of the Peace. It is possible that Cromwell thought he would be appointed one of Huntingdon's aldermen, and he was therefore resentful when he was passed over. Things were not easy for Cromwell anyway – his rich and powerful relatives had left Hinchingbrooke so the Montagus were the new political force in town. In 1631 Cromwell sold all of his property in Huntingdon and moved to St Ives.

Civil War

When Cromwell returned to his birthplace, in April 1643, it was as a colonel in the

The charter of 1630. (County Record Office Huntingdon. Huntingdon Borough Charter No.17)

Parliamentarian army, leading a force of 2,000 foot soldiers and 10 troops of horse and dragoons. The Civil War divided the loyalties of many towns, and Huntingdon was no exception. Huntingdon's position within the area held by the Eastern Association did not mean that every one of its inhabitants was a Parliamentarian. Indeed, even members of Cromwell's own family fought for the King: his uncle Sir Oliver, for example, raised large sums of money for the King's forces, while Sir Oliver's son John, born and baptised in Huntingdon, begged Cromwell in 1649 to spare the King's life. The warm welcome given to Charles I when he arrived in Huntingdon in 1645 shows how highly the ordinary townspeople thought of their King as well.

Huntingdon would have seen much military activity during the years 1643 to 1645, as troops frequently marched through the town, and new defences were being built near the bridge. To prevent a surprise attack across the river during the Civil War the fourth arch from the northern end of the bridge was demolished in 1645, and a drawbridge put in place instead. The arch was rebuilt after the war was over. The site of the old Norman castle, overlooking the river, was refortified with gun batteries.

These fortifications turned out to be useless, as the attack, when it occurred, came from the north. A few weeks after the battle of Naseby, while Cromwell and Fairfax were away preparing for an attack on Bristol, Charles I and his forces attacked Huntingdon. On Sunday 24 August 1645 a Royalist army marched south from Stamford and took a Parliamentarian force near Stilton by surprise, before quickly moving on to Huntingdon itself. Parliamentary troops tried to organise the town's defence but it was too late. After a short skirmish the town fell. At 5.00pm on Sunday afternoon Charles himself arrived in Huntingdon, where he received a warm reception from the town's Royalists. The news of Huntingdon's fall, however, prompted the other Parliamentarian forces in the area to rally, so the Royalist army withdrew on Tuesday 26 August before any serious fighting could start. The Royalist army, which included Oliver Cromwell's cousin, Colonel Henry Cromwell, took money, arms and hostages with them when they left.

Oliver Cromwell. Portrait attributed to Robert Walker. (Cromwell Museum: HUTCM/110)

It is a popular local belief that the battle of 24 August damaged many of Huntingdon's buildings, and that the churches of St John's and St Benet's in particular were blown to pieces. However, recent research suggests that the actual fighting was limited. It seems more likely that the town's churches fell down through deterioration and neglect. There is also the possibility that some damage was inflicted deliberately by Parliamentarian iconoclasts charged to destroy superstitious images, such as William Dowsing, appointed by Edward Montagu, second Earl of Manchester and a relative of the Hinchingbrooke Montagus. No churchwardens accounts survive for Huntingdon's parish churches, so the full extent of

The Barley Mow in Hartford, built using stone from St Benet's Church following its demolition in 1802. (The authors)

the destruction of mediaeval glass and artwork is not known: but iconoclasts are known to have visited the county.

Oliver Cromwell's last wartime visit to Huntingdon had been in May 1645, and as far as anyone knows he never returned. Certainly he did not return while he was Lord Protector. Charles I, however, did pass through the town again. Hinchingbrooke had hosted many royal visits from 1603 onwards, but the royal visit of June 1646 was the last for many years. During his removal from Holmby in Northamptonshire to Hampton Court, Charles spent one night at Hinchingbrooke, guarded by Parliamentary commissioners. Colonel Montagu's wife, 'with a feeling that did honour to her sex and station', treated the captive king with respect, protecting him from abuse and insults.

The Civil War may not have brought much actual fighting to Huntingdon, but it severely damaged the town's economy, by disrupting communications and transport, and causing taxes to rise. The people of Huntingdon spent the post-Civil War years reconstructing their town and rebuilding their lives. The town remained in a bad way for many years after the war. A grant of 1663 described Huntingdon as a 'poor decayed town, which being on a frequented road was greatly impoverished by the insolencies of armies, free quarters etc during the late wars'. When Charles II visited Huntingdon in 1664 he was reportedly pleased that Oliver Cromwell's home town was in such a ruined state, and he took his own revenge on Huntingdon by shooting at the bridge during his barge journey along the river. Huntingdon's future looked bleak.

CHAPTER 3

'An Air of Quiet Regularity': Prosperity in Georgian Huntingdon

THE TOWN that we see today is largely a Georgian creation. Huntingdon prospered during the 18th century, but this success was not won easily. Possession of a mediaeval market charter was no short cut to economic success. No longer was it enough to out-perform St Ives and St Neots: Huntingdon now had to compete with new manufacturing and spa towns. Yet Huntingdon's population rose remarkably during this period. From an estimated population of about 1,188 people in 1674, it rose to 1,235 in 1705, then to about 2,000 by the end of the 18th century, and finally reached 3,267 in 1831. A 'town gentry' developed in Huntingdon, who built new houses, developed new businesses, and led the recovery of Huntingdon's fortunes. England's old chartered towns had to fight as hard as the new ones for their share of the market, and it is to Huntingdon's credit that, despite its small size, it not only managed to survive, it grew.

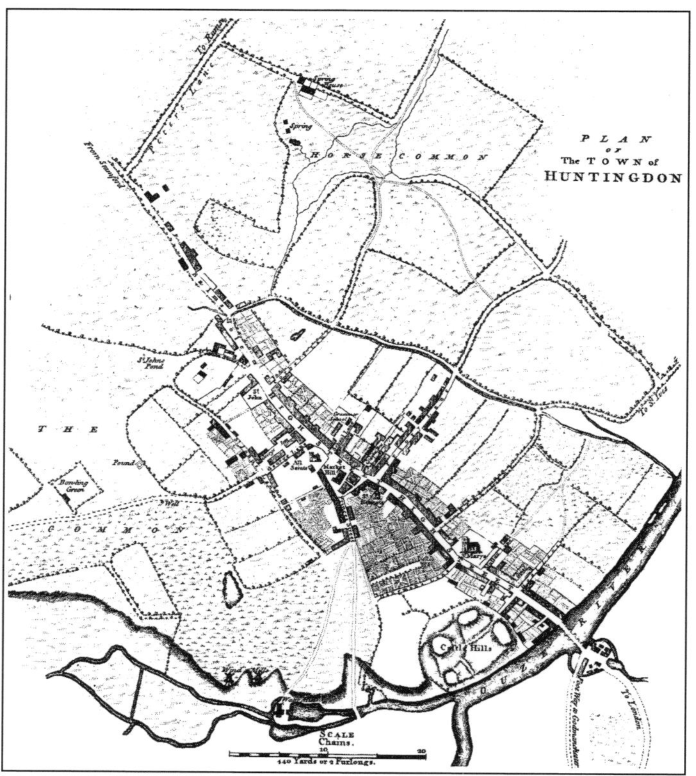

Map of Huntingdon, drawn by Thomas Jefferys in 1768. (Huntingdon Library)

Turnpikes and taverns

Georgian Huntingdon owed at least some of its economic success to the growing wealth of the countryside around it. Drainage of the nearby fens, completed by 1665, meant that more land was under cultivation, which in turn led to greater prosperity. Another factor lay in Huntingdon's excellent transport connections with London. London accounted for about 11 percent of the British population: it contained almost one million people by the end of the century, which made it the largest city in Europe, twice the size of Paris. Eighty percent of all imports into Britain went through the London docks. This affected all the other towns and cities in the south and east of England, Huntingdon included. They changed from being local centres into being subsidiaries of the national capital, supplying London with new people and taking its goods and following its fashions. Even its newspapers came from London. Not until 1813 did Huntingdon get its own newspaper, *The Huntingdon, Bedford and Peterborough Weekly Gazette*; and for the first two years of its life even this newspaper was printed in London, and had to be brought up to Huntingdon by stagecoach. Economically and culturally, Huntingdon was becoming more and more dependent on traffic and trade from the capital.

Huntingdon benefited from its position on the Ouse and on the Great North Road. The 17th and 18th century saw a great improvement in the quality of English roads. In 1674 John Ogilby published *Britannia*, the first road atlas in Britain. The road north through Huntingdon was one of the very first in England to be 'turnpiked': in 1710 a private trust put up the money to repair and maintain the road, and in return the trust was granted the right to charge tolls on road users. Drainage ditches were dug, stones were laid down to make a permanent road surface, and sections were widened. A gate or 'pike' was placed across the road, which had to be opened to allow access: hence the name 'turnpike'. By the end of the 1750s the cross-country routes had been turnpiked too – Huntingdon's townspeople could travel easily along turnpike roads to Biggleswade, Newmarket, Cambridge, Oundle and Market Harborough.

Huntingdon became fashionable. There was now even a licensed London-style coffee house, run by John Fisher, where customers gossiped and gambled. Coffee houses offered tea and chocolate, as well as coffee, and were very popular, despite coffee's reputation for being an anti-aphrodisiac. Most travellers, however, would have visited one of the large number of inns and public houses which existed along the new turnpike roads. A list of inns in Huntingdon borough, dating from 1765, lists 22 pubs, some of which still exist today (The George, The Falcon, The Three Tuns) but the names of others have long since vanished: The Bull and Dolphin, The King of Prussia, The Duke of Cumberland, The Spread Eagle. This 1765 list is hardly comprehensive – it fails to mention The Fountain Hotel, for instance, where the town's magistrates themselves often met to hear cases. There were possibly many more.

The two main coaching inns were The George and The Fountain. The George is first mentioned in the 1572 town survey, but it only really took off with the coming of the coach trade. Much of the present courtyard dates from the late 17th century, and in the early 18th century the two-storey stable ranges were added at the rear,

The Fountain Hotel, photographed in 1890. The premises were later acquired by Murkett Brothers and used as a garage. The building was sold during the 1960s and is now Woolworths. (County Record Office Huntingdon: MC4/16/3)

backing onto George Street. During the 1820s four coaches bound for London departed The George every day: the *Regent*, the *Perseverance*, the *Boston Mail* and the *Wellington*. Two more London-bound coaches, the *Boston Mail* and the *Edinburgh Mail*, left each day from The Fountain Hotel, an imposing red-brick building constructed during the 18th century. Other coaches served routes from Huntingdon to Peterborough, York, Boston, Scotland, Northampton, Leicester, Stamford and Cambridge. As well as ale, food, and rooms for travellers to sleep in, these large inns offered entertainments like skittles, dominoes and cockfights. These inns also served as centres for news and gossip as well as being used as local trading centres for the sale of commodities like wool or grain by sample rather than in bulk.

Huntingdon's inns also offered prostitutes to their travellers. This was the era when Barnaby Rich famously wrote that a good pub would offer him ale, tobacco and a 'pocksy whore', all for 3d. Huntingdon, perhaps because of its position on the Great North Road, seems to have had more prostitutes than just one to each pub. During the reign of William IV (1830–7) Huntingdon's 'red-light district' was centred on The Sun and The Windmill pubs, both situated at the southern end of the High Street near St Mary's Church. In April 1831 both pubs were raided and seven prostitutes were arrested 'for the reception and entertainment of travellers' – Mary Fields, Maria Stephen, Susan Reid, Maria Fuller, Mary Rose, Elizabeth

Hilliam and Mary Ann Cropley. They were all sentenced to 11 days' imprisonment, quite lenient by the standards of the day.

Crime and poverty

The inns brought crime, too. In 1825 John Thong, a farrier, assaulted Thomas Hillyard in the yard of The Falcon Inn, following 'Hillyard's remarks on the bad character of Thong's wife.' At the same time George Woodward, a labourer, was indicted for getting drunk and assaulting town constables John Bushell and John Richardson. The minute books of the Borough's magistrates are full of cases of assaults, petty theft, vagrancy and drunkenness. In December 1811 the *Old Cambridge* stagecoach was held up on the stone bridge. Many of these crimes were committed by outsiders, rather than by local people: the perpetrators came from as far away as London, Lincoln and Northampton, as well as from the surrounding villages. In 1798, six soldiers were employed to search out the 'footpads' who had been terrorising the town.

The old prison in Orchard Lane. The window at ground level is the original cell window. A new prison was built in St Peters Road in 1829. (The authors)

Criminals faced a variety of punishments. Some were publicly whipped: Elizabeth Currey was ordered to be flogged in 1763 by the Huntingdon assizes for 'stealing goods to the value of 10d' and Sarah Mason was similarly lashed in 1773 for stealing some buckles and buttons. Some criminals were branded, on the heel of their left thumb, while others were incarcerated in the town's prison. This was a cramped building on the junction of the High Street and Orchard Lane. Criminals on capital offences were kept in irons, and the keeper was allowed to increase the weight of the irons if he thought further punishment was necessary. There were no separate cells for inmates, just two large rooms, one for men and one for women.

Huntingdon's citizens are known to have worried about what effects such mixing of prisoners would have on the minds of first-time offenders. 'Without due classification of prisoners, what improvement can be effected in their moral condition?' asked Robert Carruthers in 1824: 'if a boy of 12 or 14 years old, committed for some petty larceny, be compelled to associate freely with rogues and highwaymen who have grown grey in the commission of crime, and whose conversation is chiefly made up of narratives of their past exploits, is it not obvious that he will return to society rooted and confirmed in those bad habits?' Such concerns seem surprisingly modern. A new prison was built in 1829 on St Peter's Road, paid for by the county, and the one in Orchard Lane was closed.

The worst criminals were executed. Between 1751 and 1800 at least 54 people were sentenced to death by the assizes sitting in Huntingdon, including two women and a 13-year-old boy. Most of these sentences were commuted to transportation to the American Colonies (or to Australia, after the American War of Independence), but almost a dozen people are known to have been hanged on the gallows on Mill Common.

Many people committed crimes because they were poor. Several of the wealthier residents were willing to act to help their fellow townsfolk, but, as in every town or village, they would not help those from outside. In 1783 Susannah Rawlings was expelled from Huntingdon and ordered to return to her home town of Dartford in Kent. She was so ill that she was carried in a cart as far as the town's boundary. Help was available, though, for those living in the borough. In 1710 George Lysson bequeathed £50 to set up a charity 'to provide bread for the poor of St Mary's parish'. Ten years later Thomas Woodward arranged for 10 shillings to be spent each year on bread for the parish's poor; in 1817 Henry Sweeting gave £100 for bread, too. Some of the conditions of these bequests seem rather specific. The £20 bequeathed by Henry Blaine in 1796, for example, was only to be spent 'amongst the poor of Mutton Lane'.

'The lamentable effects of superstition'

Many of Georgian Huntingdon's population were nonconformist. Nonconformist attitudes had already existed *within* the English Church until the 1660s – the Church of England had managed to include people of such different religious views as Oliver Cromwell and Charles I, for example – but this situation changed after the 1660s, when the Act of Uniformity excluded Protestant noncon-

Sketch by George Tytler showing the town of Huntingdon from Spring Common, 1817. (County Record Office Huntingdon: accession 1398)

formists from religious rites and from government positions. In theory, nonconformists were not allowed freedom to worship until 1689, but the Assize Rolls for Huntingdonshire tell a different story. In 1682 four magistrates of the county were themselves presented at the assizes 'for not suppressing conventicles and not putting the Laws into Execution against absentees from the parish churches'. They were William Donce, Mayor of Huntingdon, Sir Nicholas Pedley, recorder of the town and Sir Lyonall Walden and Thomas Harris, Justices of the Peace for Huntingdon. With them under the same charge were 14 constables and about 260 private persons.

There were numerous groups of dissenters in English society, including Presbyterians and Unitarians, but Huntingdon's nonconformist community was largely Congregationalist and Baptist, traditionally made up of lower middle-class people. There was nothing really radical about these groups. In the 1740s, Methodism became popular among disaffected evangelical Anglicans: Huntingdon's Methodists set themselves up in a barn off Castle Lane, and it was here that John Wesley preached to them in 1780. Only in 1811 did they build a new brick chapel for themselves in the High Street. The Baptists and Independents clubbed together to build a small chapel, the Union Chapel, on Grammar School Walk in 1823. The Quakers moved between individual members' houses, before finally settling down near St Clement's Passage, on the south-eastern side of the High Street. No new Anglican churches were built in Huntingdon. The remains of old St Benet's were finally pulled down in 1802; plans to demolish All Saints and St Mary's churches, and replace them with a single new one, were dropped.

Beliefs and attitudes even within the established church were changing. The beginning of the Georgian era had seen an old-style execution for witchcraft, when Mary Hickes and her nine-year-old daughter Elizabeth were condemned to death by the assizes and were hanged in Huntingdon on Saturday 28 July 1716. Enlightened spectators at the execution despaired that such 'lamentable effects of superstition' should still exist in Huntingdon. Over time these progressive views prevailed. Huntingdon's traditional sermon against witchcraft, given

The Union Chapel in Grammar School Walk, built in 1823. The chapel was later used as a school, and subsequently became the County Record Office. (County Record Office Huntingdon: WH9/12A)

every Lady Day in All Saints Church following the Witches of Warboys case in 1593, carried on throughout the 18th century but was quietly dropped during the reign of George III. The last preacher we know of is W. Panchen, who gave the sermon on 4 May 1814. After that, the money was spent on bread and coal for widows instead.

'In a flourishing condition...'

The Georgian era brought prosperity to Huntingdon. In 1745 its inhabitants raised £2,059 13s 10d towards crushing the Jacobite rebellion, hardly a negligible sum. In November 1775 the borough proposed a loyal address to the King, supporting him on the outbreak of the American War of Independence: the Earl of Sandwich had 'sustained considerable loss' by the American rebellion, 'particularly by the confiscation of a landed property in South Carolina, consisting of eighteen thousand acres'. In 1782 Admiral Sir George Rodney defeated a Spanish squadron of ships and, to mark his victory, he was given the Freedom of Huntingdon, possibly at the instigation of the 4th Earl of Sandwich who was First Lord of the Admiralty: the borough raised £55 for a gold box in which to keep the parchment recording the grant.

The 4th Earl had another, longer-lasting legacy. He was widely believed to be a heavy gambler, and a story even circulated among the Georgian gentry that he had once sat for 24 hours at a gambling table eating only salt beef between slices of bread. The idea of using slices of bread to wrap a filling quickly caught on, and the word 'sandwich' was in use to describe such a meal by the 1760s.

Literacy levels in the town were high. A study of signatures in the marriage registers of Huntingdon's two parish churches during the period 1790–9 shows that 60 percent of its inhabitants could sign their own names, pretty much the national average for urban areas (Halifax had a literacy rate of 60 percent, too, for example). This was a far higher level of literacy than the surrounding villages could claim: Alconbury, for instance, had a literacy rate of 29 percent, and Kings Ripton had just 21 percent.

The high level of literacy in Huntingdon was due to the excellent educational provision there. The town was no longer solely dependent on the old Grammar School. In 1719 Lionel Walden bequeathed £500 to the town 'for the building of a Free School', for 20 boys who could not afford the Grammar School fees. The school finally opened in 1736, following legal wrangling. In 1760, a Leicestershire landowner called Gabriel Newton gave £26 a year 'towards the clothing, schooling, and educating of twenty five boys of indigent or necessitous parents of the established Church of England'. The money was used to clothe the boys at the Walden School in green coats, hence the school coming to be known as the 'Green Coat School' – a tradition still carried on today with the green uniforms at Hinchingbrooke School.

Sketch of the Grammar School in 1845. During the Georgian period other schools began to compete with the Grammar School, which went into a decline. (County Record Office Huntingdon: MC4/14/6)

In 1813, a National Boys' School was built on the corner of St Peters Road and Ermine Street for 175 children. The school was supported by donations and voluntary subscriptions. The Grammar School itself, meanwhile, seems to have gone into something of a decline. Its masters tended to be second-rate clergymen who let the curriculum fall into decay.

Some of Huntingdon's better educated inhabitants became doctors. All English towns during the Georgian period suffered from outbreaks of smallpox, typhus, influenza, tuberculosis, measles, and diphtheria. But instead of responding to these epidemics with superstition, educated Georgians began to study them, and to work out ways of at least limiting their effects, even if they could not be completely cured. In 1763 Huntingdon surgeon William Smith was given the body of Ramsey murderer Richard Keen, 'to be dissected and anatomised'. In 1793 the

Huntingdonshire Medical Society was set up: its minute book shows that Huntingdon had nine medical experts (three physicians and six surgeons and apothecaries), while Peterborough only had six, and St Neots had just two. Huntingdon's smallpox and cholera cases were isolated in the Pest House on Spring Common.

A dispensary was built in 1789, opposite Mill Common, funded by public subscriptions and donations. By the 1820s it was seeing nearly 400 patients a year, and had invested in state-of-the-art medical technology, such as a 'Vapour Bath and Electrifying Machine'. In 1831 Revd John Fell, rector of All Saints, offered a house rent-free for a year, so the infirmary could be enlarged to accommodate in-patients. A matron was appointed on £25 per year to run the new infirmary.

This literacy allowed a level of cultural activity far beyond what villages could supply. In 1782 the county's Justices of the Peace paid Ann Jenkinson, bookseller, for binding four of their volumes – the going rate was 2s 6d per book. During the 1820s there were at least three rival booksellers in Huntingdon. Alexander Peterkin was one of them. He felt the need to supplement his income from time to time: in 1818, for example, he took on the duties of collecting the town's taxes, and in 1831 he pleaded with the magistrates to allow him to be the sole supplier of their stationery. But many traders had several different lines of business at the time, and Peterkin was at least well off enough to afford a portrait of himself.

The educated townsfolk could subscribe to libraries and book clubs, too. In 1742 a book club was set up in The George, its members dining together every month. The bookseller Mr Wood established The Ladies' Book Society, which met in his shop. This proved so successful that he followed it up with the Huntingdon Book Club. Bookseller Mr Lovell followed in 1817 with his own Huntingdon Literary Society, which met in the rooms above his shop. Not

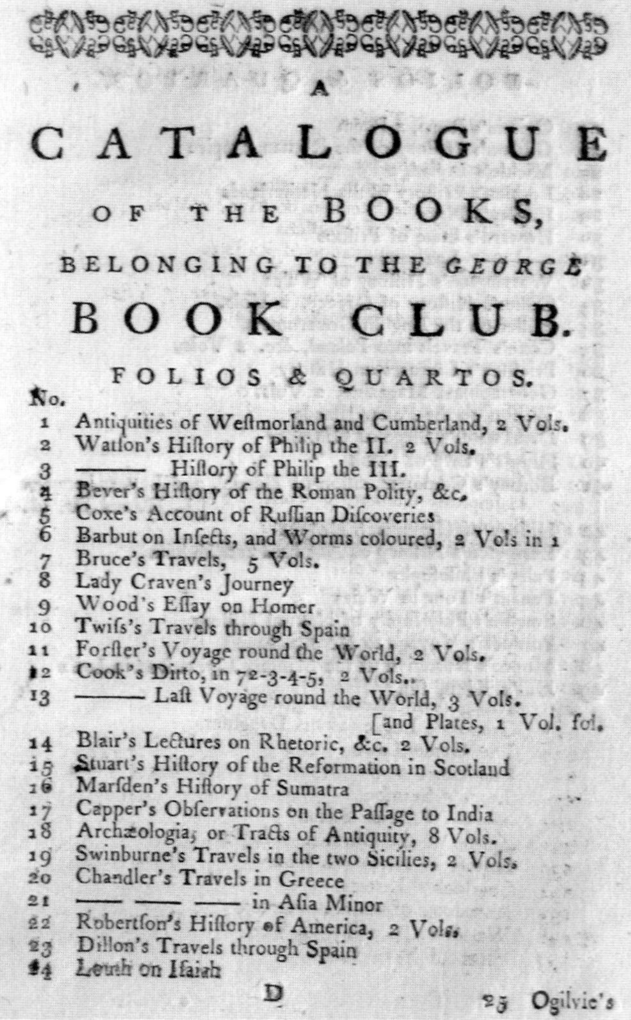

A

CATALOGUE

OF THE BOOKS,

BELONGING TO THE *GEORGE*

BOOK CLUB.

FOLIOS & QUARTOS.

No.

1 Antiquities of Weſtmorland and Cumberland, 2 Vols.
2 Watſon's Hiſtory of Philip the II. 2 Vols.
3 ——— Hiſtory of Philip the III.
4 Bever's Hiſtory of the Roman Polity, &c.
5 Coxe's Account of Ruſſian Diſcoveries
6 Barbut on Inſects, and Worms coloured, 2 Vols in 1
7 Bruce's Travels, 5 Vols.
8 Lady Craven's Journey
9 Wood's Eſſay on Homer
10 Twiſs's Travels through Spain
11 Forſter's Voyage round the World, 2 Vols.
12 Cook's Ditto, in 72-3-4-5, 2 Vols.
13 ——— Laſt Voyage round the World, 3 Vols. [and Plates, 1 Vol. fol.
14 Blair's Lectures on Rhetoric, &c. 2 Vols.
15 Stuart's Hiſtory of the Reformation in Scotland
16 Marſden's Hiſtory of Sumatra
17 Capper's Obſervations on the Paſſage to India
18 Archæologia; or Tracts of Antiquity, 8 Vols.
19 Swinburne's Travels in the two Sicilies, 2 Vols.
20 Chandler's Travels in Greece
21 ——— ——— ——— in Aſia Minor
22 Robertſon's Hiſtory of America, 2 Vols.
23 Dillon's Travels through Spain
24 Lowth on Iſaiah

D 25 Ogilvie's

The George Book Club catalogue. (Huntingdon Library)

to be outdone, Alexander Peterkin set up a 'general circulating library' instead. In 1824 Carruthers proudly noted that 'these institutions are all in a flourishing condition, and evince the increasing spirit of enquiry and intelligence which pervades the town and its vicinity'.

The courtyard of the George Hotel. During the Georgian period this was not just a popular coaching inn, but also an important meeting place for the town's educated classes. (Huntingdon Library)

Reading was not the only pastime. After 1745, monthly balls and assemblies, with dancing, tea drinking and card playing were held in the new Town Hall. On 8 November 1832 the Town Hall was the venue for a dinner for 280 people, followed by a ball, and fireworks on the common; all to celebrate the coming of age of the 7th Earl of Sandwich. Groups of actors visited The George to stage plays and comedies, and a theatre was built in 1801 on the corner of George Street. Horse racing took place on Portholme Meadow from 1750, being compared favourably with the racing at Derby by Horace Walpole in 1760. The Corporation improved 'The Walks' by planting trees along the roadside to create a pleasant and shady walkway from the town to Portholme. A bowling green was laid out near Hinchingbrooke House.

There was also a new and growing awareness of the town's history. Robert Carruthers, a 25-year-old 'well informed and ingenious Scotchman' who worked

Huntingdon High Street looking towards St Mary's Church, with Cowper House on the right. (County Record Office Huntingdon: PH48/75)

for a few years as a teacher in Huntingdon, diligently noted all the archaeological discoveries which had been made in the town. Some human bones, for example, had been uncovered on the premises of Mr Tipping, a coachmaker living on St Germain Street: these suggested to Carruthers that the site of the mediaeval church of St Germain had been found. Skulls and other bones were also unearthed in Mr Cowell's Close, in All Saints parish; and 'great quantities of bones' were dug up in William Newell's garden in St Mary's Lane. Carruthers carefully wrote down all these facts in his book, *The History of Huntingdon from the Earliest to the Present Times*, which was published in 1824. Carruthers later returned to Scotland, where he became editor of the *The Inverness Courier* and helped edit the first edition of *Chambers' Encyclopedia*.

'Many elegant houses...'

The 18th century was a period of considerable building activity in Huntingdon. The new found prosperity meant that many residents were able to replace their old houses with the latest designs. Huntingdon was becoming a model Georgian town. William Cowper, who lived there between 1765 and 1767, described Huntingdon as 'one of the neatest towns in England'.

New shops, inns and coffee-houses were constructed along the High Street and around Market Hill; older tenements were refronted or extended. Lionel Walden,

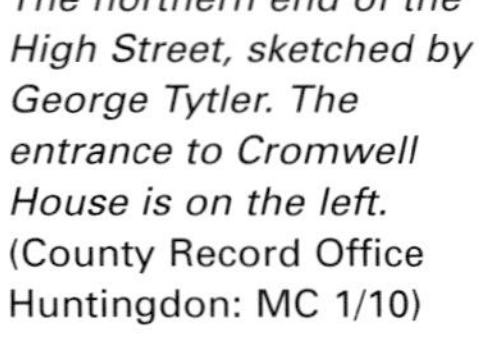

The northern end of the High Street, sketched by George Tytler. The entrance to Cromwell House is on the left. (County Record Office Huntingdon: MC 1/10)

Cowper House. It was here that the poet William Cowper spent the years 1765–7, living with his friend the Revd Morley Unwin. The topmost window in the middle is a fake one: it is really just brickwork painted to look like a window. Cowper House now houses the offices of The Hunts Post. (Huntingdon Library)

the town's MP in 1661, 1679 and 1685, was probably the builder of Walden House, an elaborately decorated red-brick house on Market Hill. Huntingdon's other wealthy families were not to be out-done, however. Building started at the fashionable northern end of the High Street, away from the noise and bustle associated with the river. In 1727 alderman Edward Audley built Whitwell House right at the top of the High Street. By 1728 a branch of the Ferrar family of Little Gidding built Ferrar House, next to St John's churchyard. The large red-brick house built about 1720 opposite the Hartford Road junction, now called Cowper House after the poet who lived there between 1765 and 1767, was as far south as fashionable building went at this time.

Slows Cottages, built in 1796 and demolished when the ring road was built. The church in the background is St Mary's. (County Record Office Huntingdon: 1096/17)

As the 18th century went on, the southern half of Huntingdon began to see imposing new buildings as well. The Margetts built Orchard House next to the gaol. In 1787, the

Castle Hill House. Built in 1787 by Oscar Rowley, the house had extensive grounds which included much of the site of the old castle. Archdeacon Francis Vesey lived in the house from 1874 until his death in 1916. The site of the castle was presented to the town in 1918 in memory of Archdeacon Vesey. (County Record Office Huntingdon: PH48/81)

Rowley family built Castle Hill House, opposite St Mary's Church, whose grounds included the site of the former castle. In 1796 cottages with three storeys (a rare architectural feature in a cottage), called Slow's Cottages, were built at the bottom of St Clement's Passage. By 1800 a large house adorned with a Robert Adam-style doorway had been built next to the river, today's Old Bridge Hotel.

Even the shops changed. The old open windows were replaced by fashionable new barrel-shaped glazed ones. Haggling over individual sales was replaced, too, by the new trend of quoting a fixed price for all customers – which encouraged quicker sales and allowed a more accurate forecasting of profits.

The Old Bridge Hotel, formerly a private house. (The authors)

The focal point of the town, however, was the new Town Hall. The old 16th-century structure was severely damaged by fire in 1743; only its staircase was rescued and was re-used in a new town hall erected in 1745. The new building was built in brick but the walls were stuccoed and painted in imitation of Portland Stone, to emulate the more imposing buildings elsewhere in Georgian England. There must have been some problems with it, as the borough's officials often continued to meet in the local inns – it has been suggested that the building was too draughty. In 1817 an open colonnade was added for traders to use, and a second-floor tea room was added to the Assembly Room, which was decorated with chandeliers, mirrors, and expensive paintings, including a Gainsborough portrait of the 4th Earl of Sandwich (who had contributed £500 towards the cost of building the new Town Hall), and a full-length portrait of Queen Caroline, wife of George II.

Not all the new buildings met with universal approval. The theatre, built on

The Town Hall, as it appeared in 1824. This engraving shows the open loggia on three sides, built in 1817. At this time the whole façade of the building was whitewashed. (Huntingdon Library)

George Street in 1801, was considered by some to be rather ugly: Carruthers wrote that its 'exterior is mean and inelegant'. But enough Georgian architecture survives in Huntingdon for us to see that Huntingdon would have been an attractive place to live. Carruthers thought that, overall, 'the general appearance of Huntingdon to a stranger is highly pleasing and prepossessing. The principal street is spacious... over the whole town is spread an air of quiet regularity, neatness, and comfort, seldom found in larger and more populous places. If it lacks somewhat of that stir and bustle usually expected and prevalent in the chief borough of a county, it contains none of those exterior signs of squalid want and wretchedness which tread fast on the heels of splendour and profusion...'.

William Cobbett, a visitor to the town, was equally impressed. 'Huntingdon is a very clean and nice place, contains many elegant houses, and the environs are beautiful', he wrote in *Rural Rides* (1830). 'All that I have yet seen of Huntingdon I like exceedingly: it is one of those pretty, clean, unstenched, unconfined places that tend to lengthen life and make it happy.'

The Assembly Room in the Town Hall. (County Record Office Huntingdon: PH48/288/2)

More symbolically, by the end of the Georgian period Huntingdon was also lit. Gas was first supplied to Huntingdon in 1832. A gasworks was built next to the river,

Market Hill in 1852, dominated by the gas lamp. (County Record Office Huntingdon: MC4/1 6/2)

at Mere Dyke wharf. Artificial lighting was not a simple utility: it was a scientific wonder, and a constant reminder to Huntingdon's 3,000 townspeople of the benefits of urban living and successful trade. At the dawn of the Victorian era Huntingdon's future was – literally – bright.

CHAPTER 4

'In the service of the Empire': Victorian and Edwardian Huntingdon

THE VICTORIAN period started well. Following the Municipal Corporations Act of 1835, and despite the objections of town clerk George Frederick Maule who wished to see the continuation of the political *status quo*, Huntingdon's old undemocratic borough council, which had been in place since 1630, was swept away and replaced by a new representative body with an elected mayor and councillors. Poor relief was placed in the hands of elected Guardians too; a new workhouse, incorporating state-of-the-art thinking about social architecture, was built on St Peter's Road. In 1840 the buoyant nature of the market and the stagecoach routes encouraged the borough to improve the Town Hall and the Market Square. The town's prospects looked bright.

Yet none of these changes fundamentally altered the social base of political control in Huntingdon. The introduction of democratic elections was an attempt to open up borough politics to new people, but Huntingdon's power struggles still involved the same old families; the membership of the town's elite hardly changed. Parliamentary elections were fought between members of aristocratic families who had lived in Huntingdon or the surrounding area for generations. At the beginning of Victoria's reign Huntingdon's social, political and economic world revolved around the activities of the Montagu family, living in Hinchingbrooke House: 80 years later, in 1914, the Montagus were still there, and they still called the shots.

Victorian respectability

The Montagus were *the* family to know during the 19th century. The seventh earl, John William Montagu, was an aide-de-camp to Queen Victoria, and colonel of the 5th Battalion King's Royal Rifle Corps; Edward Montagu, the 8th earl, served as the borough's MP for the years 1876 to 1884, became the first chairman of the new Huntingdonshire County Council when it was created in 1889, and served on diplomatic missions to Constantinople, Berlin and St Petersburg. Not only did the

Edward Montagu, the 8th Earl of Sandwich, photographed in 1890. (County Record Office Huntingdon: WH1/110B)

family sit at the heart of the town's politics, they were central to its economic and social life, too. It was unthinkable to set up a respectable new society or organisation in the town without inviting the Montagus to lead it. There was a Huntingdon Cycling and Athletic Club, and a Huntingdon Angling Association: the Earl of Sandwich was chairman of both.

In many ways the Montagus' commitment to the needs of Huntingdon's inhabitants was genuine. In 1876 Huntingdon suffered from severe flooding. Earlier failure to clear obstructions from the river from Houghton up to Brampton had caused much of the problem, and some of Portholme meadow's tenants petitioned the Earl to lend his support to a river clearance scheme. The Earl need not have bothered to do very much at all, but he actually responded by setting up a Huntingdon Flood Committee, and carefully watched the progress of the River Conservancy Bill though Parliament, even sending copies of the bill to interested parties for their comments and support. In 1880, when the cost of new river management schemes for the town were estimated to be £1,600, the Earl contributed the first £500.

Around the Montagus moved Huntingdon's upper middle classes, who indulged in typical Victorian intellectual and leisure pursuits. In 1840 Godmanchester surgeon Robert Fox established Huntingdon's own Literary and Scientific Institute, which moved into plush purpose-built premises on Huntingdon's High Street in 1842 (the building is now the Commemoration Hall). Fox's aim was to bring

A view of Portholme, showing the floods of 1875. The building in the background is the racecourse grandstand, designed by Robert Hutchinson. (Norris Museum: PH/HUNTN/053)

together the town's scientists, surgeons, manufacturers and merchants, and thereby create an exciting atmosphere in which radical new ideas could be created, supported and discussed. The fact that rooms were dedicated to smoking, chess and billiards suggests that the Institute's appeal was not wholly intellectual, however. Its subscription fees were £1 for gentlemen and 10 shillings for ladies, although even this membership charge would have been beyond the reach of many people. By 1877 the Institute boasted a library of 2,400 volumes and even a 'collection of curiosities and of philosophical apparatus' that had once belonged to Fox himself.

An 1842 sketch of the Literary and Scientific Institute, founded by Robert Fox. The original statue of Minerva, the Roman goddess of wisdom and the arts, was made of bronze: the statue visible on top of the building today is a modern fibreglass replica. (County Record Office Huntingdon: MC3/4/9)

Sport occupied much of Huntingdon's middle classes' leisure time. Rowing, 'pedestrianism' (athletics), football and cricket all became fashionable. As early as the 1840s there were two informal, pub-based cricket clubs in the town – Huntingdon Albion Cricket Club and the Huntingdon Victoria Cricket Club – which played their matches on the 'turnip piece' on St Peters Road. By 1869 the Marshall Brothers brewery had paid for the erection of a pavilion there, and in 1880 a proper town cricket club was formally established. The Earl of Sandwich, naturally, was invited to be the club's first president (the Earl had his own private cricket ground at Hinchingbrooke, anyway). Huntingdon also boasted its own golf club.

Some of these sports, including golf and croquet, became fashionable with middle-class ladies. Lawn tennis was especially popular during the late Victorian period as it was one of the few areas in society where women were allowed to abandon their heavy skirts in the presence of men. Other women joined Huntingdon Ladies Hockey Club, which existed from 1897.

Bicycling became popular after the 1870s, so popular in Huntingdon in fact that the town's celebrations marking the end of the Boer War in 1902 were in the form of a fancy dress bicycle pageant, and the 1911 Coronation party included a bicycle parade. Murketts even made a bicycle for ladies

2

THE READING ROOM

IS SUPPLIED WITH :

Daily.	*Weekly—*
Times.	Cambridge Independent Press.
Daily News.	Beds Advertiser.
Daily Telegraph.	Stamford Mercury.
Standard.	Peterborough Advertiser.
Morning Post.	Hunts County News.
Pall Mall Gazette.	*Monthly.*
St. James' Gazette.	Art Journal.
Globe.	Magazine of Art.
Echo.	Nineteenth Century Review.
Weekly.	Chambers' Journal.
Illustrated London News.	Cornhill Magazine.
Graphic.	Good Words.
Illustrated Sporting and Dramatic News.	English Illustrated Magazine.
Punch.	Leisure Hour.
Fun.	Sunday at Home.
Judy.	Cassell's Family Magazine.
Moonshine.	Longman's Magazine.
Liberal and Radical.	Quiver.
Cambridge Chronicle.	Bradshaw's Railway Guide

And Numerous books *for reference only.*

3

THIS INSTITUTION PROVIDES, IN ADDITION TO THE READING ROOMS,

BILLIARDS,
CHESS,
SMOKING
AND
MUSIC ROOMS.

The Subscriptions are payable in advance as under :

		£	s.	d.
Annual Members	Ladies ...	0	10	0
	Gentlemen ...	1	0	0
Quarterly Members	Winter Quarters (each)	0	2	0
	Summer " "	0	1	6

The Institution is open from 9 a.m. to 10 p.m. to Annual Members, and from 5 p.m. to 10 p.m. for Quarterly Members.

The benefits of joining the Literary and Scientific Institute. (Huntingdon Library)

Huntingdon Boat Club, 1892. (County Record Office Huntingdon: WH3/1053)

A garden party at Hinchingbrooke House about 1892, showing the tennis courts on the lawn. (County Record Office Huntingdon: WH3/14 12)

called the 'Hunting Don'. Huntingdon Cycling Club was a very active one, and had its own racetrack on St Peter's Hill. The town's Cycling Club would later form the nucleus of the Hunts Cyclists Battalion.

The architecture of Victorian Huntingdon

Much of what we see of today's town is due to the designs of Victorian architect Robert Hutchinson, who had a greater impact on the appearance of Huntingdon's buildings than any other single individual before or since. By the time of his death in 1892 Hutchinson had worked on all manner of buildings in the town, from the militia barracks to a new lodge at Hinchingbrooke House, and from pubs like The

Trinity Cycle Club, 1896. (County Record Office Huntingdon: WH3/1830)

Swan Tavern, on which Hutchinson worked in 1868, to workers' cottages in Newtown. Hutchinson was originally a London man but moved to Huntingdon in 1852 where, aged just 24, he set up his own architectural practice in All Saints Passage. Not only did he become the Earl of Sandwich's architectural agent, but he also became Borough Surveyor, Diocesan Surveyor, and, in January 1866, Huntingdonshire's very first County Surveyor. Most of his designs show a clean and elegant simplicity, very modern by the standards of mid-Victorian architecture, yet he also knew how to incorporate classical or Gothic elements if his clients demanded it.

Robert Hutchinson's house in Princes Street, 1880, showing the meat market in the background. (County Record Office Huntingdon: WH3/1496)

The Grammar School after its reconstruction in 1878. (Norris Museum: PH/HUNTN/045)

Acting as the Earl of Sandwich's agent Hutchinson drew up the plans and specifications for the town's new Corn Exchange, built in the courtyard of the Fountain Hotel, which opened on 3 December 1862. Hutchinson's design consisted of a hall 65 feet long and 34 feet wide, with an open-timbered and glass roof, and with a gallery at one end. In 1865 and again in 1887 Hutchinson worked on alterations to the Town Hall. In 1878 the old Grammar School building was reconstructed following Hutchinson's designs: the work was paid for by Dion Boucicault, whose son had been killed in a railway accident at Abbots Ripton two years earlier.

Hutchinson also redesigned the Church of England chapel of St John the

Evangelist in January 1873. This had been built in 1845 on the site of the old Georgian theatre, and was the brainchild of devout Church of England worshipper Lady Olivia Bernard Sparrow, who wanted to see it used by the navvies then engaged on making the Great Northern Railway. Sadly her chapel ceased functioning within weeks of her death in 1863. In 1873 the Church of England finally decided to consecrate the building, and they called upon Hutchinson to rework the building's interior. Hutchinson also worked on the nearby Hartford parish church. Both All Saints and St Mary's churches had substantial work done on them during the late Victorian and Edwardian eras, not by Hutchinson, but by architects who were considered less 'modern': St Mary's parish employed Sir A.W. Blomfield to restore and reseat their church in 1876, at a cost of over £2,000, while Gothic architect Sir George Gilbert Scott, designer of the Albert Memorial, worked on All Saints. The new Trinity Church was designed by John Tarring. The building had space to seat 850 worshippers, some schoolrooms, a library, and a spire 181 feet high, which symbolically towered over the two Anglican churches. It cost £12,000 to build, much of it raised by Potto and Bateman Brown, of the Brown and Goodman milling company. A further £1,000 was spent on an organ in 1885.

The town's Methodists on the other hand were slightly more modest: their new chapel, built in the High Street in

St John's Chapel, built in 1845 at the behest of Lady Olivia Bernard Sparrow, and reworked by Hutchinson in 1873. (County Record Office Huntingdon: PH48/117)

Trinity Church, built on the High Street in 1867–8 and shared by Baptists and Congregationalists. It was demolished in 1967, and a new Trinity Church was built on the Oxmoor estate. (County Record Office Huntingdon: PH48/13)

The laying of the foundation stones of the Methodist Church, 1878. (County Record Office Huntingdon: WH3/1085A)

1878, was a brick building accommodating just 500 worshippers. This too was a Hutchinson design. Bateman Brown was now Mayor of Huntingdon, and laid a foundation stone for the new Methodist chapel on 22 May 1878. A second foundation stone was laid by the Mayor of Godmanchester.

Hutchinson worked for businesses, too. The High Street façade of the George Hotel, built 1865–8, is entirely Hutchinson's work, and he did the basic designs for new buildings at Huntingdon gas works. The new racecourse grandstand on Portholme was also his design.

Hutchinson died in 1894, aged 66. He was buried in Huntingdon town cemetery, the very same cemetery that he himself had laid out, and whose chapel of remembrance he had designed, 40 years earlier.

Social improvement

One of the greatest differences between the Victorian era and those preceding it was a new economic, rather than just social, awareness of class. Karl Marx himself mentioned Huntingdonshire in his 1867 book *Das Kapital*. In a passage dealing with poverty Marx noted that some workers in Hartford – a village which would be absorbed into the town of Huntingdon, in 1931 – had to sleep up to eight in each room. Many of the cottages did not have toilets: instead families had to use their outdoor allotments, 'or use a closet with a trough set like a drawer in a chest of

The George Hotel, photographed about 1920. Its façade was designed by Robert Hutchinson. (County Record Office Huntingdon: WH2/43)

drawers'. Marx noted glumly that even in backward countries 'the cyclical movement of the conditions of human life proceeds more cleanly and decently than this'. Such conditions were commonplace in the poorer areas of Huntingdon, east of the High Street around St Mary's Church.

However, mid-Victorians prided themselves on the fact that, through hard work and education, individuals could rise through the classes. They had faith in the virtues of competition and the free market, in the importance of diligent work, and in the value of a strong personal morality. Successful Victorians saw their task as the 'improvement' of those beneath them, through better education, social welfare, temperance, and the control of workers' leisure time.

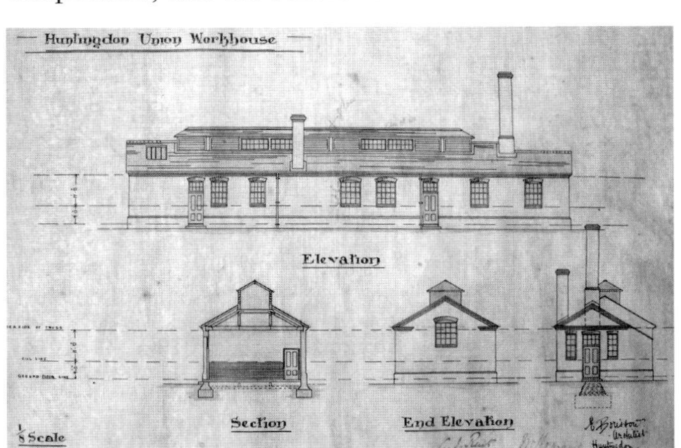

Architectural elevations of a proposed extension to Huntingdon Union Workhouse, originally built in 1837. (County Record Office Huntingdon: map 178)

The centrepiece of this social policy was the workhouse. The new Union Workhouse, which covered 33 parishes in and around Huntingdon, was situated on the corner of St Peter's Road and Ermine Street, and was completed by 1837.

The existing workhouse in St Germain Street, as well as workhouses in Godmanchester, Ramsey, Alconbury and Brampton, were phased out during July and August 1837. The workhouse was said to be of 'plain but substantial character', designed by a hitherto unknown architect called Sampson Kempthorne on a cruciform plan which gave the advantage of exercise yards between the wings. It was designed to accommodate 230 paupers, but in 1853 the average daily number of inmates was only around 130. The average weekly expense of keeping a pauper at this time was 2s 6d. The workhouse was run by a Board of Guardians, made up of local dignitaries who met regularly to discuss workhouse matters. The Huntingdon Board of Guardians met every Saturday at noon. The workhouse in Huntingdon was said to be one of the best run in the country and, like many workhouses, was not as bad as many people today believe. Food was very plain, but the three meals a day were better than many outside the workhouse had to sustain them. Cleanliness was a high priority, and everyone was expected to take a bath every Saturday.

Most of those in the workhouse were the old and infirm, particularly elderly men. Old women tended to stay with the family to help cook, clean and tend the children; men were less useful. There were also a large number of children, most of whom were orphaned or abandoned, while others were illegitimate children of other inmates. The other significant group of workhouse inhabitants was unsupported women: deserted wives, widows with children and 'fallen women' (unmarried mothers, prostitutes and those who had lost their place in society). The rest were a shifting population to whom the workhouse was the temporary solution to a crisis. Workhouses tended to fill up in winter and empty in summer when jobs were plentiful. The workhouse would be a last resort for families because they were forced to split up, with men and women being accommodated separately. The workhouse also accommodated tramps and migrants in the Casual Ward. Their clothes were washed and they were given a bath, but they were considered less deserving than the 'settled poor' so their diet was inferior, and consisted of bread and water for supper. They often had to sleep on straw and were sent on their way next morning without breakfast.

The new Grammar School buildings, erected in 1901–2. The school was taken over by the County Council following the 1902 Education Act. (Huntingdon Library)

There were occasional treats in the workhouse, however; the local papers often carried stories of events paid for by local benefactors. Christmas in the workhouse at Huntingdon (by then renamed Walnut Tree House) in 1910 is typical of many. 'Throughout the wards and day rooms the pretty festoons of coloured paper, evergreens and Christmas mottos made the interior bright and pleasant... On Christmas Eve 'Santa Claus' in the person of Miss Meadley... made a round of the children's wards and... filled

The chemistry laboratory in the new Grammar School buildings, partly funded by a grant of £250 from Huntingdonshire County Council. (Huntingdon Library)

their stockings with toys, oranges and sweets. Sunday was observed in the usual manner, the festivities of Christmas being postponed until Monday. At breakfast there was a distribution of buns, sweets and tobacco, and at lunch those who wished to have beer were supplied... out of 69 entitled to beer only 25 asked for it. The great event of the day was the Christmas dinner served in the large dining hall at 12.30... the table covered with snow white cloths and embellished with flowers, plants and bonbons groaned under an abundance of good things... roast beef, roast mutton and pork cut from the primest joints... to be followed by steaming plum pudding decked with holly, mince pies etc. All the staff appeared to delight in making the dinner a success.' The announcement of the names of those who had contributed to the festivities was greeted by cheers from the inmates.

In 1913 workhouses became known as Poor Law Institutions. The structure of the Victorian Poor Law was finally dismantled by the Local Government Act of 1929, after which the workhouses became Public Assistance Institutions.

Education was another key part of social reform. Huntingdon St Mary's National Girls and Infants School was built in 1842 on Walden Road near The Walks, and was enlarged in the 1850s. Another new infants school was set up on St Germain Street in 1867: the National Boys School, originally on the junction of Ermine Street and St Peters Road junction, joined them there in 1872. In 1870 Trinity Free Church established a mixed British School, large enough to accommodate 420 children, in their old chapel building on Grammar School Walk. This entire school later moved to brand new buildings at Brookside in 1906.

Victorians understood the benefits of literacy, and from 1850 towns were allowed to levy a rate to pay for a public library, as the cheapest form of insurance against social unrest. Nevertheless most libraries were still set up by forward-thinking private benefactors. In 1897, when the Earl of Sandwich set up the Montagu Working Men's Club, he endowed it with

Brookside School. After the school's closure in 1957 the building was used as a music and drama centre. It was finally demolished in 2001. (Huntingdon Library)

The Montagu Working Men's Club, set up in 1897. (Huntingdon Library)

a lending library of 300 books, as well as its own billiard room, reading room and bar. By 1914 the library had grown to 500 volumes and a bowling green had been laid behind the club.

Education and social welfare did not stop crime, however. Huntingdon's prison, originally built in 1828, soon had to be enlarged. In 1850 a new wing was added to the prison so that it could hold up to 124 prisoners, and it was now so large that it needed a staff of eight to run it – the governor, a matron, a chaplain, a surgeon, three warders and a night watchman. Behind the 18ft high perimeter wall were three prison blocks radiating from a central building: male prisoners were incarcerated in the north-west and north-east wings, and female ones in the south-west one. During the night of Wednesday 15 December 1847 seven prisoners broke out, including two local men, 23-year-old Robert Pewtress and 29-year-old Edward Wilson, both burglars. Security was not improved by the new building; in fact, it was even easy to break into the prison. In 1863 two women, Elizabeth Wilson and Harriet Hayes, broke in and stole money from the prison offices. Lessons about security were not learned, as in 1869 another woman, Ann Black, managed to break in and steal some money too. The prison came under Home Office control in 1877 and was finally shut down in 1892, whereupon all the prisoners were transferred to Bedford.

Huntingdon Gaol in St Peters Road. This photograph shows the new wing added in 1850. Parts of the gaol may still be seen in St Peters Road. (County Record Office Huntingdon: DC 140)

Following the Police

Act of 1856 the borough constables were incorporated into a new Huntingdonshire County Constabulary, based at the police station on the High Street. The station was never big enough for the new force, and in 1881 the constabulary moved to Ferrars Road, where the town police station still stands.

The health facilities in the town were gradually extended and improved. In 1853 a new Town and County Hospital was built on Mill Common; it was extended in 1863, and in 1898 an operating theatre was added. An Isolation Hospital in Primrose Lane was erected in the same year, and in 1902 a separate building for the treatment of smallpox cases was built a mile north of the town.

Dennis Fairey, imprisoned at Huntingdon County Gaol at the age of nine. Born in Ellington, Dennis was living in Huntingdon in 1877 when he was arrested for stealing a loaf of bread and some fruit, six days before Christmas. He was sentenced to 21 days hard labour and four years at a reform school. This photograph is from the the Gaol's register of Habitual Criminals. (County Record Office Huntingdon: 4440/368/89)

The Town and County Hospital on Mill Common. (County Record Office Huntingdon: PH48/55)

The coming of the railway

The first railway line to reach Huntingdon was built by the Lynn and Ely Railway Company, which extended its track westwards from St Ives as far as Godmanchester bridge in August 1847. On 11 August 1850 the Great Northern Railway opened its own station in Huntingdon, on the main line from London to Peterborough. The first train to travel north from the town carried about 400 guests in 17 carriages. The *Illustrated London News* reported that 'the train left London in gallant style dashing through numerous tunnels at amazing speeds of anything up to 30 miles an hour – and no doubt raising qualms in the breasts of some of the more timorous passengers.' In June 1864 the Midland Railway opened its

The Pest House, built on Spring Common for the treatment of smallpox cases. (County Record Office Huntingdon: PH48/85)

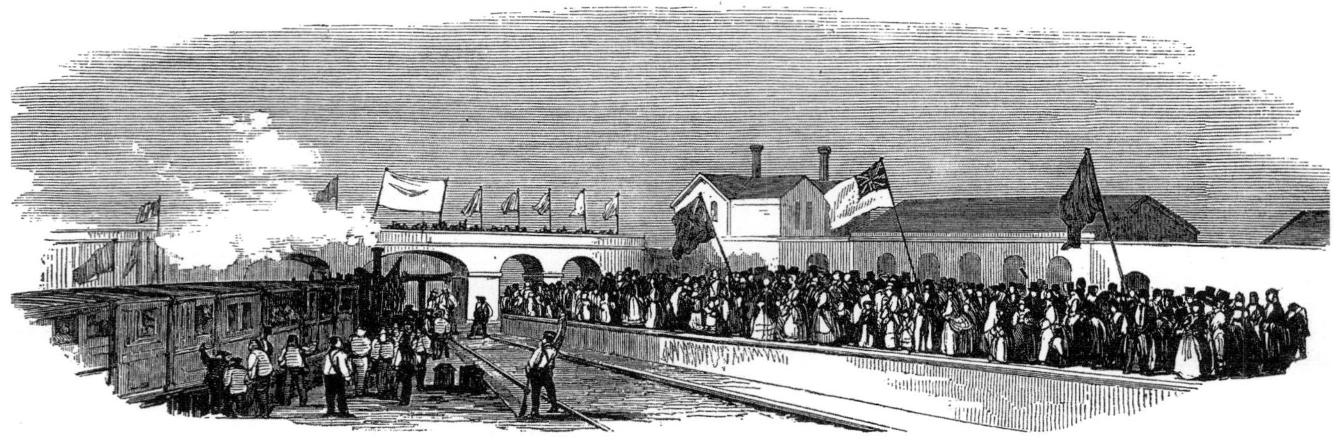

The opening of the Great Northern Railway station at Huntingdon in 1850. (Huntingdon Library)

Kettering to St Ives and Cambridge line, which helped link the town into the midlands network, and to the already-existing Eastern Counties line running to St Ives and Cambridge.

The coming of the railway was not the well-organised, well-coordinated project it is sometimes made out to be. The railway network around Huntingdon was built up piecemeal over many years. It was not until 1883 that a quarter mile of track was laid down to connect Godmanchester and Huntingdon North stations: until then passengers had to take a horse-drawn coach through the town to make their connections. The cross-country railway network was so poor that in 1849 and 1850 the trains running between St Ives and Huntingdon were pulled by horses. The timber trestle bridge which carried the line across the river and the flood plains did not help reliability either: it was subject to weight and speed restrictions, and occasionally caught fire from the sparks and ashes thrown out by the locomotives.

The Montagu family had always been opposed to railways. A number of railway companies had approached the Earl of Sandwich during the 1840s with proposals to lay track across his land, but they all failed. The only reason that the St Ives to Huntingdon line managed to get built in 1847 was that it terminated in Godmanchester, neatly avoiding any of the Hinchingbrooke estate.

Even after he had bowed to the inevitable, and had allowed the GNR to build its new station in 1850, the Earl of Sandwich still held out against further development of the railway. The borough council, keen to create new employment in Huntingdon, tried to persuade the GNR to build their new carriage works on Views Common: but the Earl did not want to have the noise of the carriage works so close to his Hinchingbrooke estate. (Even the 1850 station itself had been built where the land dips down, so the Earl did not have to see the trains.) So the GNR built their works at Peterborough instead.

The impact of the railway on the town's economy is hard to assess. Huntingdon's innkeepers, for example, were not as badly affected as some recent books have stated. *Pigot's Directory* of 1830 recorded the existence of about 20 taverns, inns or public houses in the town; by 1854, four years after the railway opened, there were still 21 pubs recorded; in 1869 there were still 21. Most people using the stagecoaches would have stayed only at the three largest inns – the George, the Fountain and the Crown – as these were where their horses were stabled. Huntingdon's other pubs always relied on locals for their custom, and so would not have been hard hit by the coming of the railway.

But the railways did bring about the destruction of the long-distance stagecoach routes. Now that express trains could travel from London northwards to Lincoln and York within one day there was no need anymore to stop off overnight at Huntingdon. Within a year of the opening of the mainline station, the Great Northern Railway was running seven trains every day on weekdays, and twice a day on Sundays. The stagecoaches simply could not compete with the level of speed or capacity. Stagecoach drivers saw their livelihoods disappear. Only four years after the opening of the station, in 1854, *Hatfield's Directory* was complaining 'the railway has completely destroyed this kind of business, and deprived them of the support and traffic consequent thereon.'

But many people in Huntingdon welcomed the railway. Former agricultural labourers now applied for jobs with the railway companies: a job on the railway paid well, relative to agriculture, and was secure. Forward-thinking businesses paid for railway sidings to come directly into their premises. A spur went from the Great Eastern Railway into Brown and Goodman's steam mill at Godmanchester, for example.

Capitalism in Huntingdon

Steam power had other applications besides running railway engines. In 1861, for instance, Messrs Brown and Goodman imported the latest steam technology from France for their new eight-storey high mill on the Godmanchester side of the river. The town's old brewery, which had been operating since at least 1792, was taken over by Marshalls in 1865 who then introduced steam machinery at their St Germain Street site to help create their most popular beer, I.P.A. – 'a bright sparkling beverage, exceedingly palatable, of fine tonic properties and very nutritious'. To someone standing on Castle Hill in the 1880s, a view across Huntingdon would have included many columns of steam and smoke from factory chimneys, rising into the air.

Brown and Goodman's Steam Mill, built in 1861. (County Record Office Huntingdon: PH48/77)

These new technologies affected patterns of employment. There is an excellent example of this in Huntingdon. Before 1896 individual washerwomen and laundresses, working out of their own cottages and yards, did most of the laundry in the town. The 1891 census shows that Huntingdon managed to support at least 33 such women, most of them working in the poorer labouring areas of the town, in the courts and side streets off the High Street south of St Mary's Church. They used scrubbing brushes and corrugated boards, and often worked in insanitary, unhygienic conditions. But in 1896 a new 'public sanitary laundry' was opened on Hartford Road. The Huntingdon Steam Laundry was fitted out with various modern appliances including 'a complete artificial drying outfit, rendering it independent of the season'. The Steam Laundry offered a full laundry collection and delivery service, serving markets in Godmanchester, St Ives and St Neots too. By the time of the 1901 census many previously self-employed washerwomen were now employed at the laundry: no doubt they still worked just as hard as before, but the profits from their labour went to businessman Thomas Swann, rather than to themselves.

A failing town?

Huntingdon at the end of the 19th century was a small, traditional market town, populated with lower middle-class workers – shopkeepers, bank clerks, teachers, local government officials – and operating at the centre of a largely agricultural county. Its economy was not built on industry, but was based instead on a small number of family-run businesses, on a handful of professional services, and on the administrative functions which came from its position as county town, the seat of local JPs, the centre of a registration district and poor law union.

What the town needed was large-scale industry, but it never quite managed it. An attempt was made to set up a large brickworks near the railway line in 1886, but it could not compete with the even larger brickworks just south of Peterborough. Hopes were raised in early 1899 when the London engineering firm Harvey and Williams Ltd bought the Victoria Foundry in Huntingdon, and promised four hundred new jobs, but it seems that the jobs never materialised. This was bad news for an area largely dependent on agricultural labour. Agricultural wages were just half of those in mining or factory work. Huntingdonshire was hard hit by the collapse of the 1870s boom in farming, with the result that the county's population was lower in 1911 than it had been in 1901. The 1870s agricultural depression resulted in the eventual death of the Huntingdonshire Agricultural Society wool fair, which had been held on Mill Common every year from 1854.

The coming of a new century

The new century brought new opportunities, however, and Huntingdon's inhabitants seized the chances offered by new technologies. The turn of the century saw motor cars become fashionable with the wealthy. Windovers Ltd started designing and building motor car bodies in the early 1900s. The 1903 Motor Car Act allowed speeds of up to 20mph. Huntingdonshire County Council started registering vehicles and issuing number plates. Meanwhile Dennis and Harry Murkett, owners of

The Earl of Sandwich in his Daimler landaulette. (County Record Office Huntingdon: WH3/2261)

an old established bicycle firm in the town, grasped the opportunity to move into the motorbike business. They began to make motorbikes in 1897 and soon started to export them to Australia and Scandinavia.

Huntingdon even contributed briefly to early aircraft development, too. James Radley and Will Rhodes-Moorhouse were two keen amateur aviators who wanted to build and fly aeroplanes. The old flat horse racing course at Portholme was perfect for them – the site had been derelict since 1896, when racing moved to the new steeplechase course at Brampton – and they decided to persuade the town that a permanent aerodrome could be established there. Portholme's owners (including the 8th Earl of Sandwich, who held a meeting with his

Motor cars in Huntingdon. (Norris Museum: PH/HUNTN/018)

Portholme tenants in May 1910 to persuade them of the benefits of the scheme) offered the meadow to the borough council as long as it would be used for aviation, and in February 1911 the borough rented out a neighbouring meadow to the Philaerian Company so that an aeroplane factory could be built. Radley and Moorhouse set up their own factory at 26 St John's Street in Huntingdon, where they built their own aircraft, improving on Louis Bleriot's basic designs. For a time their company, the Portholme Aerodrome Co., did well – they even set up a flying school at the end of 1911, and experimented with cargo flights that year too – but their aeroplanes were all damaged in crashes, and in 1912 Handley Page Ltd bought the company. Radley and Moorhouse's factory continued operating nevertheless, making coachwork for motor cars.

In 1899 the town's first telephone exchange opened at 1 Priory Square, off St Germain Street. It was in the front room of the Saunders house and was operated by Mrs Florence Saunders, mother of the Mayor.

The town had realised that residential expansion would be needed to house a new and larger workforce if technological progress was to be sustained. The first houses in the Newtown area had been designed by Robert Hutchinson, on behalf of the Earl of Sandwich: the first 82 plots were auctioned at The George as early as April 1860. These early houses were built in a grid around Victoria Square, a pleasant grassed area with lime trees in front of the Victoria Inn. But it was only at the turn

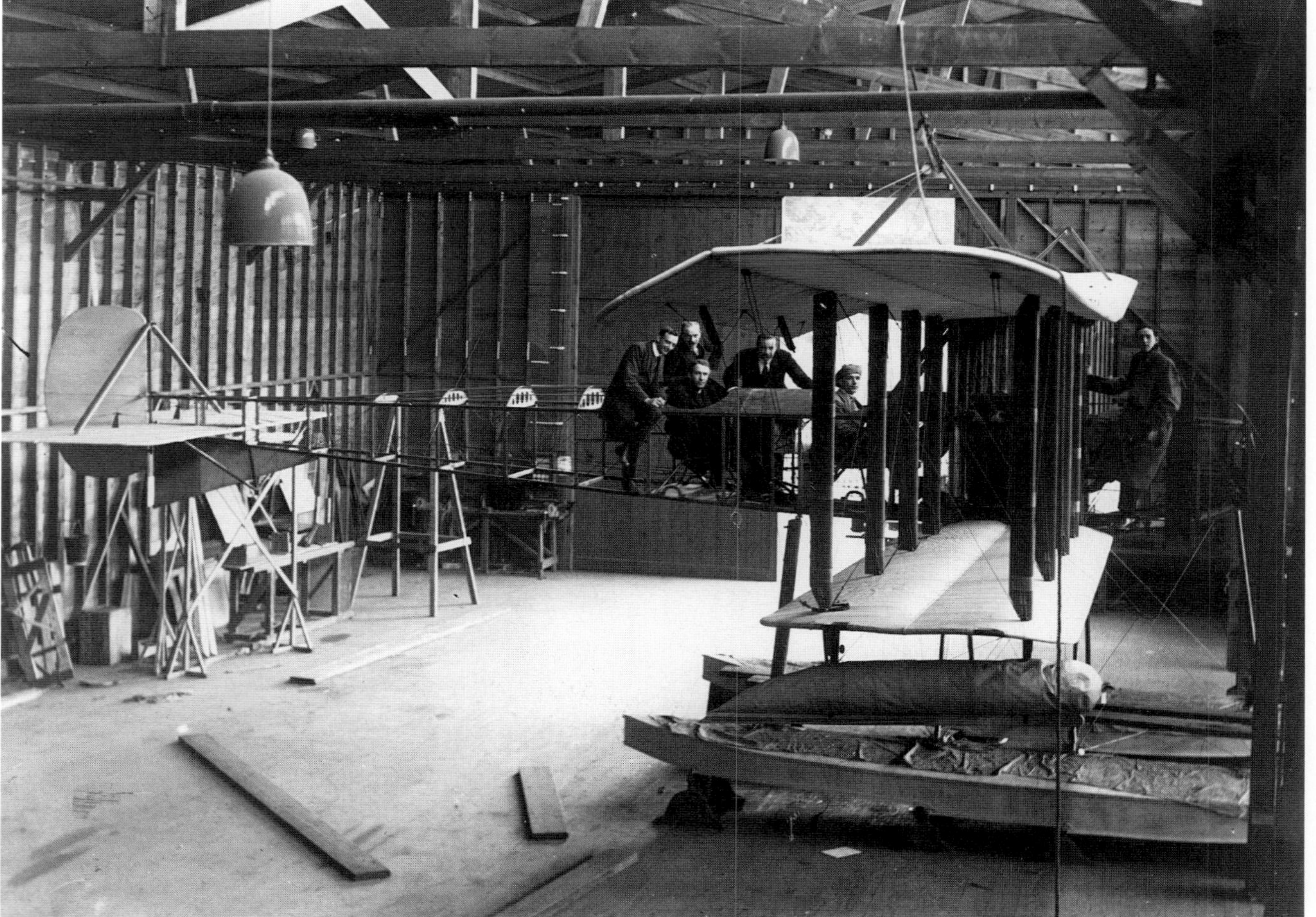

A Wright seaplane under construction by the Portholme Aerodrome Company, 1915. (County Record Office Huntingdon: WH3/2640)

Victorian terraced houses in Ouse Walk. (The authors)

of the century that Newtown's growth really took off, as hundreds of new houses were built to house Irish immigrant workers. This influx of Irish Catholics led to the building of Huntingdon's first permanent Catholic church, the Church of St Michael the Archangel, built on Hartford Road in 1901, which replaced a small iron church which had opened in 1871 at the behest of a large number of Irish cattle men who visited the St Ives market. Newtown's residents even organised their own football club.

The harsher aspects of Victorian institutionalism were eased during the Edwardian period. The 1908 Children's Act, for instance, abolished imprisonment for juveniles under the age of 14, and proper juvenile courts were created. In Huntingdon, St Edwards' Boys' Home on Mill Common was established by the Earl of Sandwich to house 21 boys from 'poor circumstances': it opened to take its first boys in July 1905.

New entertainments arrived, including Huntingdon's first cinemas. When Harry Murkett bought the Fountain Hotel and Corn Exchange site in 1911 he decided to convert the old corn exchange building into a cinema. Customers walked down a passage next to the Murkett Brothers garage into The Grand, which could seat about 500 people. The Grand soon had competition: the small schoolroom at the side of the old Congregationalist chapel on Grammar School Walk became the tiny Gem cinema in 1912. The Gem was enlarged the following year, and reopened to customers with the two-hour Italian silent spectacular *Quo Vadis?*

Victoria Square. (The authors)

Yet in many respects Huntingdon had not changed at all during the Victorian and Edwardian period. The Montagus were still the main political force in town. While Edward Montagu, the 8th Earl of Sandwich, sat as chairman of Huntingdonshire County Council, his nephew George Montagu was Conservative MP for Huntingdonshire's southern division 1900–6. In June 1906 the Montagus achieved the ultimate social cachet of a royal visit from King Edward VII: he made a visit to the town and stayed a few nights at Hinchingbrooke House.

The 1906 royal visit was not the only cause for excitement in Huntingdon, for the Montagus liked organising events in the town. Huntingdon's inhabitants enjoyed historical pageants in particular, celebrating the town's heritage. In April 1899 Huntingdon hosted the commemorations to mark the tercentenary of Cromwell's birth. Flags decked the High Street, a public tea was held and the original parish registers were put proudly on display. Railway companies organised special excursions to the town, with the result that a thousand people gathered at Trinity Church on

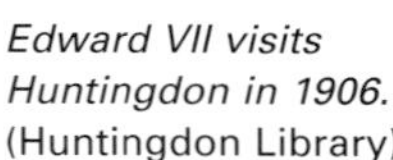

Edward VII visits Huntingdon in 1906. (Huntingdon Library)

Thursday 25 April to hear speeches and raise toasts. Nor was the Cromwell tercentenary an exceptional event. The Earl of Sandwich himself hosted several other historical pageants, such as that of 6 July 1912, with participants dressed up as Queen Elizabeth, King John, Charles II and others. But, as Huntingdon celebrated its past, the town was moving inexorably into the 20th century. The next hundred years would bring periods of hardship through the war years and beyond, and the town would see many changes, which would make it almost unrecognisable to its Victorian inhabitants.

The tercentenary of Cromwell's birth, commemorated in Huntingdon on 27 April 1899. A large crowd gathered in Market Hill to hear several speakers. (County Record Office Huntingdon: WH3/1946)

The Boer War

The Boer War, or the Transvaal War as it was referred to at the time, began in October 1899, the last war of the Victorian era. There was considerable interest in the war at home and it was covered extensively in the local press. As usual, the enemy was portrayed in a very bad light in the papers. *The Hunts Post* printed comments from a lady correspondent who had visited the Transvaal. She had this to say: 'The average Boer does not undress when he retires to rest... he is unshorn, unwashed, unbrushed; his skin, hair and clothing are all of the same hue... Among the people you see young girls looking fresh and pretty but they grow terribly fat or miserably thin with increasing age. I have seen ugly old women in different parts of

Huntingdon High Street about 1900. (County Record Office Huntingdon: WH2/91)

the world, but, beyond doubt, for utter and hopeless ugliness, the aged Dutch vrouw carries the palm. Some of these old women are more bitter against the roonieks and rooibatijies (English soldiers) than even the men, who often hate the English simply because they are English and more refined than themselves.'

In the early days of the war Lieutenant Colonel Robert Gunning was killed in action, while leading his regiment in the storming of Dundee. Between 1886 and 1891 Lt. Col. Gunning had been Adjutant of the 5th Battalion King's Royal Rifles (the Hunts Militia). He had become a familiar figure around the town, and was a friend of the Earl of Sandwich and other leading families in Huntingdon.

A considerable number of Huntingdon men were involved in action in the Transvaal, including six brothers from a single family, the children of John and Elizabeth Goodliff. This unique feat warranted a letter of congratulation from Queen Victoria, commending the family for its loyalty. Harry, Walter, John, William, George and Douglas all gave up their respective occupations and volunteered for service in South Africa. John Goodliff returned home to Huntingdon in June 1901 after being involved in 30 engagements. Another brother, Douglas, who served in the Army Medical Corps, remained in South Africa after the war. Only one of the six brothers perished, William, who fell victim to disease.

The Boers did well in the early part of the war, and the siege of Mafeking loomed large in the thoughts of those at home. At least two of the Goodliff brothers, John and William, were involved in the expedition to relieve Mafeking, and a letter describing their exploits appeared in *The Hunts Post*. Mafeking was an insignificant town on the railway line to Rhodesia, and its loss would have made little difference

A militia parade on the Grammar School field during the early 1900s, showing the barracks in the background. (County Record Office Huntingdon: WH2/254)

to the progress of the war: but the relief of Mafeking in May 1900 after a siege of 218 days led to wild and jubilant scenes across the country, not least in Huntingdon, where the celebrations were said to have exceeded those for the Queen's diamond jubilee. According to *The Hunts Post* 'one and all gave themselves up to unrestrained rejoicing and unbounded enthusiasm and the spectacle of unbridled joyousness and animation resembled a veritable pandemonium'. Flags were everywhere, even tied round the necks and legs of horses and dogs; people donned costumes which 'at other times would have appeared ludicrous and ridiculous'. Others contented themselves with wearing 'repulsive masks and long nasal appendages', while 'musical instruments of every known variety – trumpets, horns, jew's harps, tambourines, whistles etc. etc. – were employed, whilst not a few requisitioned household utensils and rattles to further demonstrate their excessive hilarity'. These

Recruits of the 5th King's Rifle Regiment outside Huntingdon barracks. The barracks building was incorporated into the Cromwell Square residential home during the early 1970s. (County Record Office Huntingdon: WH3/1940)

A group of Hunts Volunteers, 1901. (County Record Office Huntingdon: WH1/340)

celebrations were tame compared with those in St Ives, where the town pump on Market Hill, other pumps and railings from the council store yard were all destroyed in a large bonfire.

Despite the Boers' successes the English army appeared to have no respect for them as adversaries. One Huntingdon soldier, Private C.H. Johnson of the 20th Hussars, wrote to his parents that 'we don't see many of the Boers in the day time, they come in the dark, but we are always waiting and ready for them. We don't care twopence for the lot of them, they call themselves men, they may be men, but they can't fight for toffee... I don't think the war will last much longer, at least, I hope not, I am nearly fed up with it.'

Private Johnson was right. Just one month later, in June 1902, there was further rejoicing in Huntingdon as peace was announced. News of peace filtered through on Sunday 1 June, but most of the celebrations took place on Monday, which was declared a holiday by Deputy Mayor, Sir Arthur Marshall. Schools were closed, and small boys ran about letting off firecrackers, not without risk, as some boys were reported as lying on the ground trying to blow the fireworks into action! Fairy lights, flags and bands and a torch-lit procession helped the local people celebrate the end of the war.

Six Huntingdon men perished in the hostilities. In July 1901 Huntingdon witnessed a military funeral for Private Arthur Jeffs who had died in the County

Celebrations in Huntingdon marking the end of the Boer War, 1902. (County Record Office Huntingdon: WH3/2082)

Celebrations for the coronation of Edward VII, which took place shortly after the end of the war, in August 1902. (County Record Office Huntingdon: PH100B/25/1)

Hospital after returning from South Africa. In October the same year, *The Hunts Post* reported the widow of a soldier killed in South Africa having to sell a piece of Boer needlework which had been sent back from the front.

The Boer War memorial in All Saints churchyard, refurbished in 2003. (The authors)

In October 1903 a memorial honouring the Huntingdonshire men who had fallen in South Africa was unveiled. The memorial had been paid for by public subscription, and featured a copy of the statue of St George by Donatello, cast in bronze standing on a gothic base. The names of the fallen were inscribed on the pedestal. The memorial was unveiled by General Lord Grenfell. Alderman F.W. Veasey, Mayor of Huntingdon, accepted custody of the memorial with the words 'should our country ever be in difficulties, this little county would again find men ready to come forward in the service of the Empire'. Just 11 years later the men of Huntingdon were called upon to do just that.

CHAPTER 5

'Every man must take his part': Huntingdon during World War One

ON 3 JULY 1914, as they enjoyed themselves at the Elizabethan pageant at Hinchingbrooke, the people of Huntingdon can have had no idea about the horrors that awaited many of their young men over the next four years. About 550 people dressed as courtiers, pedlars, jesters, gypsies and, of course, as the Queen herself, danced and sang for thousands of spectators, some of whom had travelled from London on a special train from King's Cross. A month later the country was at war with Germany.

Elizabethan revels at Hinchingbrooke, July 1914. (County Record Office Huntingdon: accession 4231A)

Within a week of the declaration of war on 7 August 1914 the Hunts Yeomanry had been called into Huntingdon and was being billeted in public houses through the town. People returned from their holidays on the east coast; some were reportedly buying in extra food stocks in case of shortages. Army and navy reservists were called up, horses were requisitioned and the Union Jack was raised over County Hall. The 14 August issue of *The Hunts Post* was reduced in size due to fears of paper shortages caused by a North Sea blockade, but there was still room to report on the first 'spy scare' in Huntingdon, when a journalist was spotted making notes by the town's bridge.

Preparations for war continued apace through August. Lord Sandwich, the Lord Lieutenant, appealed for all men between the ages of 19 and 30 to make themselves available for the army. Mr G.H. Fowler, an expert shot himself, fitted up premises in the High Street as a miniature range for shooting practice. The old Murketts premises were transformed into a recreation centre, or 'Soldiers Institute', for use by the Territorials. In September the first contingent of 600 soldiers arrived for billeting. They were followed by the Highland Mounted Brigade, which was inspected by King George V on Portholme meadow. The King, dressed in khaki, rode across Mill Common on his own black charger that had travelled with him by train from London, and spent two hours inspecting the troops. Empty houses in the town were used to billet the troops, as were 'Corporation houses' in Ambury Hill. Large wooden buildings were erected on Mill Common, Views Common, Spring Common and in Archdeacon Vesey's paddock at Castle Hill House to accommodate the horses belonging to troops billeted in Huntingdon over the winter.

The 8th Earl of Sandwich, 1915. (County Record Office Huntingdon: PH101/31)

Answering the call

Recruiting averaged about 20 to 30 volunteers a day in Huntingdon, once the harvest was over. Between 1 and 8 September 1914 no fewer than 169 men joined up in Huntingdon; by November 1915, 400 Huntingdon men had joined up. This constituted about 10 percent of the total population of 4,003. So far only about 14 had been killed.

Nevertheless, Lord Sandwich complained of 'appalling indifference' in rural Huntingdonshire, and there was already talk of white feathers being sent to unmarried men of the right age who had not enlisted. Early in 1915 cartoons began to appear in the newspapers aimed at those who had not yet joined up, with captions such as *Daddy why weren't you a soldier in the war?* Following the Compulsion Bills of 1916 numerous cases came before the Huntingdon War tribunal of those trying to escape service. For example Victor Pentelow, a Huntingdon ironmonger, claimed that his business was a national service and that he had three brothers already serving in the army. He was granted a temporary exemption, but as the war progressed and more men were needed, he in turn was called upon to join up. Victor's younger brother Frank had already been killed in February 1915, and Victor himself was wounded right at the end of the war, while serving with the Tank Corps. He died in France on 20 November 1918, only days after the armistice.

King George V riding across Mill Common towards Portholme, 1914. (County Record Office Huntingdon: PH48/131)

Everyone was expected to do their part, even if it was as only as part of the Huntingdon Volunteer Brigade. These men practised drill and shooting every week, to enable them to be able to guard the locality, freeing others to join the army fighting in France. In January 1915 the first drill of the Volunteer Brigade was held in the new assembly room of the Huntingdon Grammar School. Volunteers included the Mayor, members of the Town Council, bank managers and the local postmaster. Field Marshall Viscount French inspected 751 members of the Hunts Volunteer

The King returns from reviewing the Highland Mounted Brigade on Portholme, 1914. (County Record Office Huntingdon: PH100B/24)

Brigade at Hinchingbrooke in 1918. He delivered an impassioned plea to all those who were classed as C category men (those who did not undertake the full amounts of drill and other duties – 339 in all). His speech was reported in *The Hunts Post* under the headline 'Grave Warning to Slackers':

> The fact of the matter is so many people in this country do not realise the gigantic nature of this war, and the terrible things which are at stake. Your whole existence as a nation is at stake – your family, your houses, your goods and property… we are engaged in one of the most terrible wars this world has ever seen and every man must take his part… unless every able bodied man in this country does realise what is going on and his duty to his country we will lose this war. You all know the consequences of that.

A group of volunteers, 1914. (County Record Office Huntingdon: PH100B/104B)

Families who had several members serving in the forces were singled out for praise by the local press. One extreme example was the widowed Mrs Cooper of St Germain Street. Her husband had fought in the Crimea and in India, and now she had eight sons, three grandsons and three nephews serving in the army. The newspaper failed to mention that her son-in-law was also in the army!

The Grammar School's assembly hall. This was where the Volunteers Brigade met in 1914. (Huntingdon Library)

In addition she had soldiers billeted at her house during the war, not all of whom were welcome guests. One of them appeared before Huntingdon Divisional Bench for stealing her son-in-law's watch. The Cooper boys served as far afield as Palestine and Gallipoli. Thomas was gassed, but survived four major battles. His brother, George, was killed at the Somme.

A second Bedfordshire Regiment was formed in September 1914 for the men of Huntingdonshire and Bedfordshire, as the 1st Beds had been sent abroad. The 2nd Beds would be used for home defence. A second battalion of Hunts Cyclists was also in training in Huntingdon, while their comrades in the first battalion were in Yorkshire – however, their life was obviously not too arduous as an appeal was made for footballs to help them pass their spare time. Lord Sandwich also placed his covered swimming baths at Hinchingbrooke at the disposal of the Hunts Cyclists recruits training in Huntingdon.

Life for those stationed in Huntingdon was not particularly harsh. On 1 January 1915 the Highland reservists were entertained to dinner at the George Hotel. Regular sports matches were arranged: on 29 January 1916, for example, a team from the 31st Hunts cyclists played football against a team from Kimbolton Grammar School – the soldiers won 11-0.

Soldiers remained billeted in Huntingdon throughout the entire war. Later in the war, when Americans were stationed at nearby Wyton in 1918, the Stars and Stripes were raised over County Hall along with the Union Jack, and Independence Day celebrations were held in Huntingdon.

Troops of the Beds Yeomanry drill near the Old Bridge Hotel in Huntingdon. (County Record Office Huntingdon: WH2/247)

News from the front

Those at home in Huntingdon probably had little idea about the true nature of the war. Newspapers were monitored to ensure that they maintained morale, so reports in the local papers were always very positive: letters from soldiers were often published, but these generally told upbeat stories. Even in July 1916, when the Battle of the Somme began, the news was far from grim. On the 28 July the Hunts Cyclists finally left for France, reportedly very cheerful, and enjoying the 'voyage over'. Week after week, *The Hunts Post* reported 'great gains' and 'war going well'. One member of the Hunts Cyclists wrote:

> It is really a marvellous war. From our position one day some time ago I had the unique experience of watching an attack. I feel it is impossible to describe it. At our distance it was merely a terrible din caused by the barrage, the swish of shells going over and the rat-tat-tat of machine guns. In the distance all one could see was volumes of smoke and dust and above there were continuous lines of puffs of white and black smoke – our barrage of shrapnel and the enemy's. After a time, back came the stretcher bearers with their loads of wounded, most of them, if not too bad, smiling at the thoughts of some respite in a Blighty hospital. And the wonder is at the very small percentage of deaths.

Stories in the press emphasised the large number of German casualties, and no mention was made of the huge Allied losses. The wounded, returning home, were said to be cheerful, and large numbers of German troops had reportedly been taken prisoner.

Spirits were kept high by news of local heroes, too. Oliver Locker-Lampson, MP for Huntingdonshire North, joined up in September 1914 even though MPs were

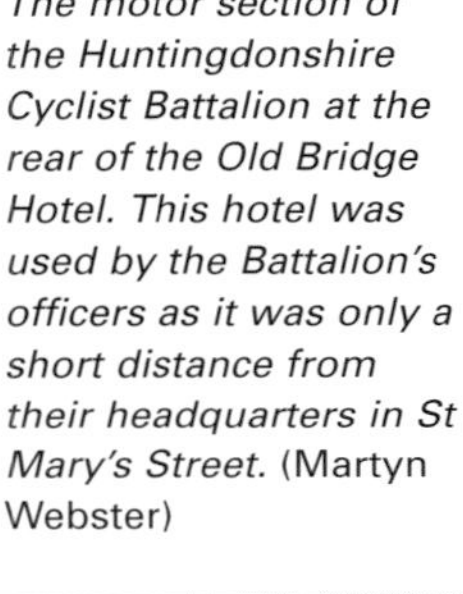

The motor section of the Huntingdonshire Cyclist Battalion at the rear of the Old Bridge Hotel. This hotel was used by the Battalion's officers as it was only a short distance from their headquarters in St Mary's Street. (Martyn Webster)

exempted from service. He commanded the Royal Naval Armoured Car Squadron and saw service in Belgium, where he was honoured by being made an 'Officer of the Order of Leopold'. Locker-Lampson's most daring exploits came in the east, however, in Romania and Russia. Local newspapers reported his many adventures and the decorations he was awarded, such as the Order of St Vladimir from the Russian Government, being made a Companion of the Most Distinguished Order of St Michael and St George by the King, and the DSO. Perhaps more tellingly, during the course of the war the Kaiser offered a reward of 20,000 marks for the capture of Locker-Lampson dead or alive.

John Hales of the Huntingdonshire Cyclist Battalion. (Collection of Martyn Smith)

Another local hero was William Rhodes Moorhouse, joint owner of the Portholme Aerodrome Company, who joined the Army Flying Corps in September 1914. Despite being mortally wounded during a mission over Courtrai in 1915 he managed to return to base with his report. For this heroic action he became the first airman to be awarded the Victoria Cross.

Most local men, however, did not have such a dramatic war as Moorhouse or Locker-Lampson. News about the horrors of life in the trenches took a long time to reach home, but civilians could guess the seriousness of the situation by the fact that war news began to take the place of advertisements on the front page of *The Hunts Post*. It was the weekly lists of casualties which gave the true picture. These lists increased in length as the war went on. Occasionally *The Hunts Post* printed letters which hinted at the true nature of trench warfare, such as this one, written from France by Sergeant Cooper in 1917 in response to news of industrial action in England:

> Only those present can understand the meaning of a murderous fire under miserable conditions such as rain and mud. Try to picture a country smashed to pieces and all the houses demolished and people driven out... You can well imagine what the boys out here feel like when they read about strikes of any kind in England. Our suggestion is to send those who threaten to strike out here and send them 'over the top'. It would brighten their ideas.

William Rhodes Moorhouse (wearing the flat cap) and James Radley with one of their aeroplanes at Portholme. (County Record Office Huntingdon: WH3/2391C)

The reality of war would have been brought home, too, by the large numbers of wounded soldiers being sent to Huntingdon's hospitals. In November 1914 the first such group arrived at the County Hospital. By March 1915 a relief hospital at Lawrence Court was receiving

Walden House, used as a hospital during World War One. (County Record Office Huntingdon: accession 4231A)

the wounded too. A Red Cross hospital was also set up in Brunswick Villas, a small house opposite the County Hospital, which opened with 10 beds on 2 September 1914. Brunswick Villas soon became too small, and the hospital moved to Walden House in December 1914. The capacity of the hospital was gradually extended with the addition of temporary buildings. By 1917 the Red Cross, or VAD, hospital could accommodate 85 patients.

Almost all the staff were volunteers, organised by Sister Birt, an Australian, who had been travelling in Germany when war broke out and who had only just managed to escape to England. The hospital received daily rations from the military authorities, but still depended largely on gifts from the local community – these were listed each week in the local newspaper and usually consisted of foodstuffs such as fruit, vegetables, eggs and cakes. The soldiers' leisure time was also taken care of. Magazines and

Dr Hicks's Red Cross group, at the rear of Walden House. (County Record Office Huntingdon: WH2/72)

books often featured on the list of donations, as did cigarettes – in May 1918 Lady Sandwich gave 1,000 cigarettes to the wounded men in the hospital. Murkett Brothers provided free transport to and from Godmanchester station. Huntingdon Model Laundry did most of the hospital laundry free of charge, and the Gem and Grand cinemas offered free admission to hospital patients on Tuesdays and Saturdays. Regular entertainments were also laid on at the hospital itself. An appeal was made in November 1917 for a recreation room to house a billiard table, and Mrs Scott Gatty, an indefatigable fundraiser, led the way by offering £50 to the fund. Within two weeks, £391 16s 11d had been raised, and Sir W. Hart-Dyke had offered the loan of his billiard table.

By the time the VAD hospital closed on 31 January 1919, 3,900 men had passed through the hospital, in addition to many hundreds of outpatients – up to 50 on one day. Almost £15,000 had been spent on the hospital: a huge achievement for a small town like Huntingdon.

The Home Front

People in Huntingdon worried about their own safety, as there was a real fear of air raids by German Zeppelins. Huntingdon could have been considered a prime target as the Bridge Hotel had become the local headquarters of the Royal Flying Corps, who had a flying field at Portholme. Plans were made to ring Windover's bell if Zeppelins were spotted. Hospitals were to show the Red Cross flag so they would not be targeted. In November 1915 the Union Guardians decided to insure the workhouse buildings against attack by hostile aircraft. Houses, businesses and shops were ordered not to show bright lights, which might attract the enemy to the town. In 1916 the use of headlights was prohibited, and in February the first motorist in Huntingdon was convicted for using lights that were too bright. John Winters of Ingram Street was fined 10s for showing a light – a fairly severe penalty, as 15s 6d was the sum for two weeks' wages for a soldier at this time.

The fear of Zeppelins was justified, as German bombing accuracy was poor and bombs intended for factories and barracks often fell on residential areas. Four people had been killed by German raids in Yarmouth and Kings Lynn. In March 1916 Zeppelins crossed Huntingdonshire on their way back from London, although no bombs fell on the county. Zeppelin reports were a regular feature in the local papers, although journalists occasionally tried to make light of the danger. In August 1916 it was reported, under the headline 'Death Caused by Zeppelin', that a rabbit had been killed on a Huntingdonshire farm after four bombs had been dropped. The rabbit, the paper reported, had later been eaten by the farmer. The same edition stated that false reports were circulating on the Continent, claiming that a quarter of Huntingdon had burned down during a Zeppelin raid.

No bombs fell on Huntingdon, however, and for many people life continued largely as normal. The local tennis club still held an annual meeting in 1916. War news took up only a small part of the newspaper columns. Fund-raising was often

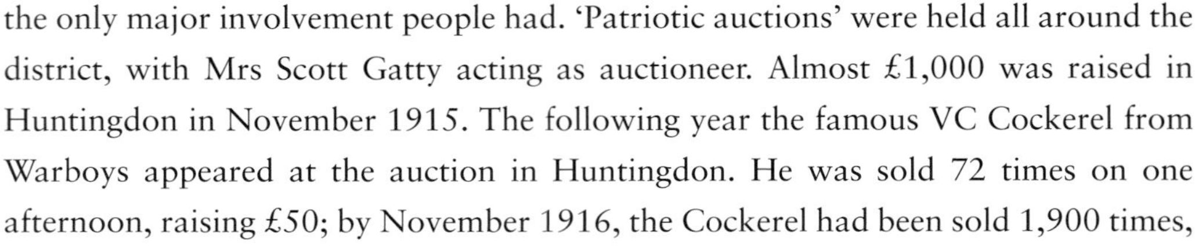

the only major involvement people had. 'Patriotic auctions' were held all around the district, with Mrs Scott Gatty acting as auctioneer. Almost £1,000 was raised in Huntingdon in November 1915. The following year the famous VC Cockerel from Warboys appeared at the auction in Huntingdon. He was sold 72 times on one afternoon, raising £50; by November 1916, the Cockerel had been sold 1,900 times, and had raised £2,080 19s 6d for war charities.

Mr Fyson with the VC Cockerel. (Huntingdon Library)

Fund-raising also went on for the Belgian refugees living in the district. There was a 'National Committee for Relief in Belgium' and the 'Star and Garter Fund' which paid for a home for disabled servicemen. Fund-raising took many forms: whist drives (often with over 80 tables), 'smoking concerts' and dances were regular events. Fêtes were often held at Hinchingbrooke, and could raise considerable amounts. In September 1917 one of the Hinchingbrooke fêtes raised £873 0s 4d for Huntingdonshire prisoners of war, Hunts War Working Parties and other charities. The workers at Portholme Aerodrome Company also organised numerous events. In April 1918 they held 'Portholme Week' with events every day – a whist drive, dance, concert at the Town Hall, football and billiard matches and a film show, which raised a total of £185.

Much of this fund-raising paid for Red Cross parcels for prisoners of war. Red Cross collecting boxes were placed in public houses, with very differing results. In 1917 the Three Tuns in Huntingdon High Street collected by far and away the most money of any pub in the county – £3 0s 5d. The other 12 pubs in Huntingdon with collecting boxes did less well: the Victoria managed 4s 6d; the Falcon 2s; the George Hotel 1s 6d and the True Briton only 7d. By the end of the war, 9,395 parcels, costing £3,755 19s 8d, had been sent off from Huntingdonshire. They could often be a lifesaver. The first prisoner of war to return to Huntingdon after the war, Signaller George Wheeler, a former St Edward's Home boy, told of appalling conditions in the prisoner of war camps. He claimed to have been kept going by the arrival of parcels from England.

As the war progressed life in Huntingdon became harder. In October 1915 shopkeepers in Huntingdon began to close their premises over the dinner hour. By August 1916 the Red Lion and Duke of Cumberland pubs in Huntingdon High Street had closed down because they were unable to find tenants to run them. Everyone was exhorted to save money. It was calculated that 15s 6d (about 77p) would pay for six hand grenades, two weeks' pay for a soldier, or two or three steel helmets, and would help to prevent economic difficulties after the war. Boy Scouts collected old newspapers. In September 1916 butter was replaced by margarine on the workhouse menu. By February 1918 there was no fresh meat for the workhouse inmates: they had to make do with corned beef instead.

The economic blockade combined with bad harvests caused food shortages and inflation. The price of wheat rose from 33s a quarter in 1914 to over 60s in 1916. During 1917 bakers were permitted to use potatoes for making bread. Bread was declared 'more valuable than money' by a speaker sent from London to urge local women to economise with food. There was even a royal proclamation printed in *The Hunts Post* urging food economy, with particular reference to grain. A committee was formed to combat waste and extravagance in the county. Dustbins were examined to ensure that nothing was being wasted: in January 1918 a total of 156 dustbins in Huntingdon were inspected, but nothing contrary to the Food Regulations was found. This had not always been the case, however. In June 1917 Charles Gadsby, a Godmanchester farmer, had been fined 10s for wasting food after bread had been found in his dustbin. The house sparrow was identified as sabotaging the war effort by consuming large amounts of grain. Local residents were urged to destroy any sparrow's eggs they could find.

Huntingdon High Street during World War One. (Norris Museum: PH/HUNTN/092)

Allotments were a valuable source of extra food. Part of Hinchingbrooke Park was dug up and used for cultivation, as were many tennis courts and private lawns, including the tennis courts at Huntingdon Grammar School, which was used for hay. Pigs and poultry were also kept at the Grammar School by the newly formed young farmers club. Housewives were urged to boil up bones and vegetable peelings to make stock. *The Hunts Post* carried an appeal for fruit stones and nutshells to be saved as they were needed by the government for 'special war purposes' – they were used to make charcoal for gas masks.

Towards the end of the war rationing was introduced. Meat, sugar, milk, coal and eventually, gas and electricity were among the items which were rationed. The local leaders in Huntingdon did their best to help. In February 1918 the 'Central Restaurant' was opened in the old grammar school buildings. It could accommodate up to 200 people and was designed to provide dinners at reasonable prices. The menu on the first day featured beefsteak pudding for 5d; rissoles 2d; potatoes 1d; greens 1d; rice pudding 2d; stewed apples 2d and custard 1d. There was no bread. According to *The Hunts Post* 'one feature of the kitchen will be to supply for home consumption tasty dishes made from wartime foods in the hope that these will induce people to enquire for the recipes and eventually make the dishes themselves.'

Women at war

Every week the Women's War Work group met under the presidency of the Mayoress, to make garments for the troops – kit bags, socks, shirts, pyjamas and jackets. Between October 1915 and February 1916 the ladies of Huntingdon sent off 688 garments. By the end of the war a total of 31,203 articles had been sent to the troops from Huntingdonshire. Children too did what they could – between 10 March and 2 June 1916 pupils from Hartford School collected 1050 eggs for the wounded.

Officers of the Hunts Volunteers, photographed outside Stukeley Hall in March 1919. (County Record Office Huntingdon: accession 2982)

By early 1916 women were being seriously considered for agricultural work, to help fill the labour shortage as many of the men had gone to the front. Most women were reluctant to volunteer. A Women's War Agricultural Committee was formed to encourage them, but it had limited success. In March 1916, 131 Huntingdon women had come forward, but only 43 were available for land work. This was still a creditable figure: St Ives and Sawtry had no female labour volunteers at all, while the 40 who volunteered from Fenstanton and Hilton were only willing to work when the weather was favourable. Things had not improved two months later, as difficulties in recruiting female labour were still being reported. During 1917 courses were run for women in agricultural skills, such as milking or rearing stock, and accommodation for the course participants was provided at Hinchingbrooke. But there were never enough women to fill the shortage, and labour had to be brought in from elsewhere. In 1917 prisoners of war arrived in Huntingdonshire to work on the land, and Boy Scouts from London were brought up to camps near Peterborough to help weed the flax fields.

One outcome of the activities of the Women's War Agricultural Committee was the formation of the Women's Institute. The institute set up for the Borough of Huntingdon in 1918 was the first of 15 in the county. The inaugural meeting was held on 26 April at the Central Restaurant and opened with an explanation of the purpose of the organisation by Lady Sandwich.

Peace at last

On Monday 11 November 1918 schools were given a holiday, bells were rung and work ceased for the day. At 4.00pm the mayor of Huntingdon finally received official confirmation of the armistice, whereupon he announced the peace from the balcony of the Town Hall. Fireworks were let off indiscriminately and there was a huge bonfire in the grounds of the Red Cross Hospital on which an effigy of the Kaiser was burnt.

Thanksgiving services were held in churches and chapels throughout the evening. National elections were held in December. Oliver Locker-Lampson, who had returned to Huntingdon as a war hero and had been adopted as MP for the united county in September 1918, was returned with a huge majority. True to form, Mrs Scott Gatty was the first woman in Huntingdonshire to cast her newly won vote, arriving at 8am, and voting, of course, for Locker-Lampson.

Celebrations were held for Huntingdon's returning prisoners of war, many of whom had not seen their families for years. Nearly 200 former POWs attended a concert and tea at the Red Cross hospital on 29 January, just before it was due to close. Mrs Scott Gatty donated badges with 'Huntingdon VAD Hospital 1914–1919' engraved on them, which were presented to all the staff, and Sister Birt was awarded a cup and £80 for her efforts. After the hospital's closure Mrs Scott Gatty had some of the outbuildings transferred to her grounds at Castle Hill House to act as a temporary hospital for disabled soldiers. The hostel was the first of its

Clayton's store at 103 High Street, decorated for the 1919 peace celebrations. (County Record Office Huntingdon: WH2/192)

kind in England, where soldiers could receive training in skills such as watch and clock making at the same time as undergoing treatment.

The Hunts Volunteers held a celebration dinner at the Central Restaurant on Wednesday 19 February. In July 1919, the formal end of the war, a 'Pageant of Peace' was held in Huntingdon, beginning with a peal of bells at 8am and at noon, followed by a united service on Castle Hill. There was a regatta, sports events, a children's tea party and a dinner for soldiers and their wives, followed by dancing during the evening. The proceedings were rounded off by the lighting of a huge bonfire on Mill Common, topped with an old aeroplane.

Discussions had been going on for some time about a lasting memorial. A memorial hall was the preferred option, the old butchers market in Princes Street being one possible site. The Lord Lieutenant wanted the memorial to be useful: he claimed it would be 'worse than useless to throw away money upon objects which in a few years, in a generation or two,

Model of the proposed new Commemoration Hall, after 1918. (County Record Office Huntingdon: DC 163)

become useless and therefore meaningless'. However, by September 1919 it was reckoned that such a hall would cost £8,000. Public subscription failed to raise anything approaching this amount. A memorial tablet in the Town Hall was proposed by the Mayor. The Town Hall memorial was unveiled on 22 February 1923 which remembered the names of 118 men and women who gave their lives between 1914 and 1918. Despite the fact that 'every effort was made to secure the names of all persons who were entitled to be recorded on the Roll... much difficulty was experienced in obtaining a complete and correct record'. Even so, it is difficult to understand how someone with such a large family as George Cooper came to be forgotten on the Town Hall Roll of Honour. The figure of 118 is obviously some way short of the final death toll suffered by Huntingdon.

The roll of honour for World War One, in Huntingdon's Town Hall. (Norris Museum: PH/HUNTN/079)

The Women's Institute, who had raised their own funds, decided to erect a war memorial in the town. The well-known sculptor Lady Kathleen Scott, widow of Scott of the Antarctic and a close friend of Lady Sandwich, was commissioned to design and make the statue. The cost of the 'Thinking Soldier' statue was met by the WI fund, although Lady Scott (or Mrs Hilton Young as she had become) charged no fee. A Mayor's Fund was opened to pay for the base and the cost of erection. Three thousand people attended the unveiling of the memorial in Market Hill by Lord Sandwich on 11 November 1923. Many wreaths and floral tributes were laid around the memorial, including one to a 'dear son' and one to a 'dear brother' laid by the family of George Cooper.

The Thinking Soldier war memorial, with floral tributes laid at the unveiling ceremony in November 1923. (County Record Office Huntingdon: MC4/3)

CHAPTER 6

'A great difference in the town's face': Huntingdon in the twenties and thirties

MUCH OF BRITAIN after World War One was gripped by widespread industrial unrest: Luton's town hall was burned down, shops were looted and smashed in Liverpool, strikes in Scotland were broken up by soldiers with tanks. But Huntingdonshire's workforce was more agricultural than industrial, and there was little appetite for militant trade union activity. The closest Huntingdon came to industrial standstill was during the General Strike, beginning on Monday 3 May 1926, when nearly every trade union member came out in support of the miners.

Huntingdon's Women's Institute, meeting in the Edward Hut near Mill Common, passed the following resolution: 'this meeting views with great distress the General Strike, and wishes to place on record the hope that the dissenting parties will soon be brought together so that the peace and prosperity of the country might be restored.' A week later, strikers in Huntingdon were using the same hut as their headquarters.

There was some disruption at Huntingdon. The Edison Bell works closed on Tuesday 4 May, and the Hosiery Mill was expected to follow shortly due to difficulties with supply. Huntingdon railway station was at a standstill on Tuesday and there were no newspapers on sale. There was a noticeable increase in motor traffic, and directional signs had to be put up in Huntingdon to ease the flow of vehicles. Eleven members of the Huntingdon Constabulary were dispatched to Ipswich on strike duty. The petrol depots at Huntingdon Station were guarded by special constables. Many railwaymen were seen on the Huntingdon streets, while others were reportedly busy on their allotments. News bulletins were posted outside the Post Office so that everyone could follow the progress of the strike.

Huntingdon Women's Institute, photographed outside the Edward Hut in 1922. (County Record Office Huntingdon: accession 4231A)

Being a predominantly rural rather than industrial town, there was little sympathy for the strikers in Huntingdon. When a miner from the Mansfield area tried unsuccessfully to obtain a lift home in Huntingdon, he was advised to take the train instead. Three ladies travelling home from Newcastle, assisted by a gentleman wearing plus-fours acting as chief guard, commented that 'the quietude of Huntingdon compared with the rowdy scenes left in the north made them realise there was no place like home'.

As usual, a committee was formed, and volunteers were called for, particularly those who could drive lorries to transport local produce. Harry Murkett was put in charge of transport. Mr Whitehead, the stationmaster at Huntingdon, was inundated with offers of help. The 9th Earl of Sandwich was one of the first to offer his services and was set to work in a signal box at Cambridge Station. The chief porter at Huntingdon was a bank clerk from London who was about to sail for Australia. As the strike wore on each day saw a gradual improvement in services. Large quantities of milk were still being sent by train from Huntingdon to London, although there was some delay in returning the 'empties'. Trains were now running through Huntingdon, although passenger services were crowded. On Monday 10 May the *Flying Scotsman* was seen passing through.

Car owners offered lifts and helped with transport, and buses came in from the villages to Huntingdon market as usual. Supplies of imported meat ran out on Saturday 8 May, but there was plenty of English meat available, and generally no shortage of food. *The Hunts Post* was still printed and distributed and, after the first few days, national papers were available too. Anthony Coote drove down to London each morning to collect the newspapers at 4am, so *The Times* was on sale in Huntingdon before 8am.

On 12 May the strike was called off unconditionally. Flags were hoisted on the Town Hall and on the churches. 'This indication of the outward joy at the defeat of an attempt by the trade unions to usurp supreme authority over the country by an illegal procedure was too galling for some local extremists, who were wont to enquire by what authority had these signs of victory been unfurled. They were reminded that the Union Jack was much preferable to the red flag.'

Building for the future

These attitudes to the General Strike reveal a streak of conservatism in Huntingdon's townspeople, particularly among the councillors who were resistant to change. When the idea of a rate-supported public library service in Huntingdonshire was first suggested by the Earl of Sandwich, in May 1920, the proposal was heavily defeated by the Council. Mr Christmas dismissed it as 'one of Lord Sandwich's pet schemes'. Mr Cordell wanted to know would they 'next be asked to provide boots and shoes and coats?' It was agreed that it was time to put a stop to such extravagant schemes. The Earl did not give up however, and by 1924 a few more members were persuaded to vote in favour of a library scheme 'provided

Aerial view of the town centre during the early 1920s. (County Record Office Huntingdon: accession 3801)

it could be done without any great expense, and by making arrangements with the Women's Institute to manage the business for them'. Alderman Tebbutt, a staunch opponent, quoted the Huntingdon Institute as being 'more interested in billiards than in the appreciation of valuable documents which were once offered to them'. Many councillors were opposed to the reading of novels, but Lord Sandwich pointed out that many councils had adopted the scheme which was found to be 'extremely valuable and not at all costly'. Accordingly, the County Council finally agreed to adopt the Public Libraries Act and become a library authority.

A library committee was formed, which met for the first time on 12 September 1925. The following year the headquarters of the new library service was established in a room 18ft by 19ft, and the first collections of books were distributed, sent out to 27 local centres throughout the county. In these early days the situation was very much one of 'beg and borrow'. An advertisement was inserted in the local newspaper asking for donations of books. One member of the Library Committee, Mr Howgate, offered the loan of his typewriter until such time as the committee could acquire one of its own, which was, in fact, eight years later in December 1934.

The new Huntingdonshire Library Service owed much to the Carnegie Trustees, and continued to benefit from their generosity. In 1931 a grant of £100 was received which was to be used for the expansion of the county centre at Walden House. This centre soon had a membership of 386, and its opening was an important stage in the development of the Huntingdonshire County Library Service.

Huntingdon's economic and social infrastructure was being renewed in a slow and piecemeal way. One of the Borough Corporation's measures, prompted by the increase in motor traffic since the war, was to improve the High Street. Until February 1936 there was a bottleneck halfway along the High Street where the premises of the Peterborough Co-operative Society jutted out into the road, causing congestion for vehicles and pedestrians. The Borough spent £800 demolishing the building and replacing it with a new one, set back to the building line. In the following year Huntingdonshire County Council spent nearly £5,000 widening the Hartford Road corner, demolishing the former vicarage of St Mary's church in the process. At the same time some old buildings adjoining the George Hotel were demolished, allowing George Street to be widened. *The Hunts Post* approved of all these changes, noting that 'people who left Huntingdon some years back will find a great difference in the town's face if they return in a year or so. There must be many more changes in the near future to cope with the ever increasing volume of traffic'.

In October 1935 the 80ft high water tower on Views Common – capable of holding 100,000 gallons of water – was filled for the first time. The new water tower was a significant improvement in the town's water supply, which until then had

The High Street, showing the Peterborough Co-operative Society building on the left. This was demolished in 1936 to widen the High Street. (County Record Office Huntingdon: WH2/77)

Damage caused by a fire on the corner of St Clement's Passage and Mutton Lane in 1924. (County Record Office Huntingdon: WH2/193)

been drawn along pipes from the river just south of the old wooden railway bridge, was at a very low pressure, and was so badly filtered as to be 'frequently turbid'. The new tower increased the water pressure threefold.

The purpose of the water tower was to improve the town's sanitation, but it had the added advantage of helping Huntingdon's firefighters, too. The twenties and thirties saw a number of large fires in the town. Bringing each of these fires under control was made difficult by the feeble pressure of Huntingdon's water supply. A massive fire destroyed the Maddox and Sons car factory in 1924, burning a car being made for the Australian Prime Minister. Four years later, in January 1928, there was an even greater fire when the Edison Bell factory burnt down in less than an hour. The factory had its own volunteer fire brigade but the speed of the fire, surging through the largely wooden factory, defeated both their efforts and those of

The new Grammar School buildings in Brampton Road.
(Huntingdon Library)

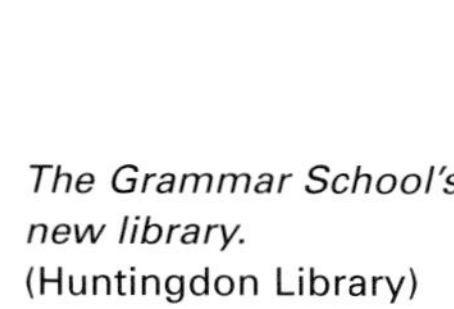

The Grammar School's new library.
(Huntingdon Library)

the borough's own firefighters. The company safe became an oven, melting the cash inside so that all the scorched banknotes became welded together. The Spring House, also known as the Pest House, was destroyed by fire in October 1931, and in July 1935 the High Street shop of Kirkham's hairdressers was gutted in a fierce blaze. This fire 'rose higher than the tall trees in Cowper-yard and lit up everywhere in St Mary's Street', according to *The Hunts Post*.

Some destruction was deliberate. In February 1927 a controlled explosion was detonated under Huntingdon's tallest landmark, the chimney of the old Falcon Brewery: over 100ft high and made of some 30,000 bricks, it had been a symbol of Victorian industry and engineering. Its demolition took seconds. The brewery had been in operation since 1814, but since amalgamation with Marshall Brothers, operations had been transferred to the more up-to-date brewery on the High Street.

Many of the town's old school buildings were demolished, too, and replaced by larger and more up-to-date premises. In 1922 the National Boys and Girls Schools merged, and in 1939 they absorbed the Infant School on Walden Road as well. Walden's Charity School moved to a new building on the Hinchingbrooke estate.

The Grammar School, in the meantime, had expanded so much during the 1920s and 1930s that it needed new buildings too. Numbers rose, and in 1920 wooden huts had to be erected as a temporary measure. Eventually a new site was found on the Brampton Road, 700 yards from the old school, opposite the entrance to the Hinchingbrooke estate. In 1938 the Earl of Sandwich laid the foundation stone and on 27 July 1939 the President of the Board of Education formally opened the new building. The new school building included science laboratories, a gymnasium, library and handicraft room and offered much more space for the 350 pupils. But within weeks the country was at war. Two gun emplacements appeared in the school grounds, and soon evacuees from London were sharing these new facilities with Huntingdon's own children.

Preserving the past

While many reminders of the past were being swept away, others were coming to light. For many years the earliest borough records were believed to have been lost, but some were suddenly and unexpectedly found in May 1939 during a survey of the Shire Hall, when the building's 'dark and dusty pigeon-holes' were cleared out. *The Hunts Post* wondered what precautions had been taken to ensure the survival of these irreplaceable parchments. John Winter, local solicitor and town clerk, replied that they would be stored in the strongroom under his office – an underground haven which extended under the pavement and the roadway, protected by 18in walls and steel doors. 'Nothing less than a direct hit could do any damage,' Winter promised.

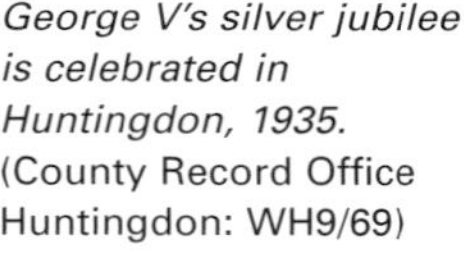

George V's silver jubilee is celebrated in Huntingdon, 1935.
(County Record Office Huntingdon: WH9/69)

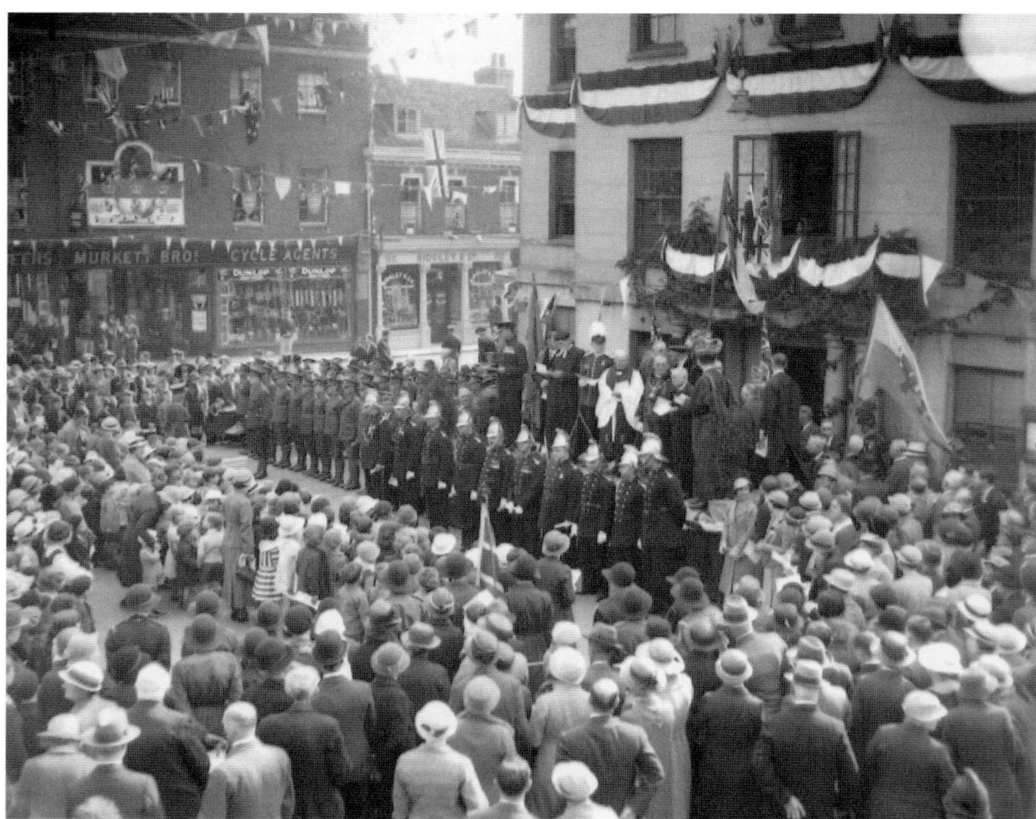

The High Street, decorated for the coronation in 1937. (County Record Office Huntingdon: WH9/77)

No one knew it at the time, but there was an even greater treasure hidden in Winter's underground bunker. In March 1941 local historian Philip Dickinson was down there looking for old documents for an exhibition for War Weapons Week when he discovered an iron safe, so old that its lock and hinges had rusted up. Using a pair of tongs Dickinson forced open the lid. Inside the safe were 14 of the earliest charters for Huntingdon – including the original charter of King John from 1205, the charter of King Charles from 1630 which named Oliver Cromwell as one of the town's Justices of the Peace, and the foundation charter of Huntingdon Grammar School. No one else had seen these records since the 19th century.

The Earl of Sandwich proposed that the town needed somewhere safe where the documents of the borough and the county could be kept at a proper temperature, and in good conditions, and he thought that the town should see that something of the sort happened after the war. In this way the seeds of the future County Record Office were sown. During the early years of World War Two, when the rest of the country was absorbed with the threat of invasion, Huntingdon was discovering its past.

CHAPTER 7

'Doing our damndest': Huntingdon during World War Two

In common with many other years, 1939 began with floods, but the people of Huntingdon had other things on their minds. While the British Government was striving for peace Huntingdon was preparing for war. The campaign to recruit volunteer fire wardens, ambulance drivers and decontamination squads had begun as early as March. Over 150 volunteers were needed: Huntingdon's response was excellent, with 135 people coming forward immediately. A government film called *The Warning*, which urged people to be prepared for the dangers of an air war, was shown at the Hippodrome for three days in June. An Anderson shelter, Bren gun and trailer fire pump were on display in the cinema entrance.

The biggest fear was of attacks by German bombers. Between midnight and 4am on the night of 13 July there was a practice black-out over the eastern counties. Wardens checked to make sure all lights were properly dimmed, and RAF planes were on duty to report the effectiveness of the test. This was followed later in the month by an exercise for the civil defence volunteers. The two telephone operators at the report centre at Gazeley House were inundated with calls, which showed that more lines were needed. An ambulance station was established at Murketts garage and a first-aid post at George Street Hall. The test was due to be repeated on 10 August, but confusion reigned when the authorities postponed the exercise for 24 hours – Huntingdon carried on with it anyway.

By the end of August 1939 air raid shelters had been prepared to accommodate a third of the population. These were at 79 Ermine Street, the Old Malthouse in St John's Street and in the extensive cellars of the Literary and Scientific Institute. Householders had prepared for the black-out: one Huntingdon shopkeeper reported that he had sold 600 yards of blind material and almost a mile of dark brown paper (black having already sold out) in just over two days. Demonstrations of respirators for babies up to the age of two years were held at Huntingdon's Town Hall and people were shown how to use a stirrup pump at Hartford playing fields. The first-aid post in the Conservative Hall in George Street now had a decontamination room in case of a gas attack. Gas detection

The former chapel in George Street became a first-aid post during the war. (County Record Office Huntingdon: DC 132)

boards were erected in various parts of Huntingdon.

Ten days after the outbreak of war the first black-out offenders were prosecuted. On 13 September, John Percival Reed, manager of the George Hotel, was fined a nominal £1 plus costs for failing to obscure all the lights on his premises. Mrs Ida Watson of 8 Ambury Road was fined five shillings after she forgot to pull the curtains over the door when she took a candle into her scullery. These fines were minimal, as they were the first offences reported: later offenders did not get away so lightly.

At 6.25pm on Tuesday 17 October the air raid sirens sounded for the first time. The streets were deserted within minutes. There was no danger, however: the sirens had gone off due to a mechanical hitch.

Into action

In April 1940 *The Hunts Post* reported that 'men from all parts of Huntingdonshire have had the honour of being members of the first territorial battalion to go into action against the Germans on the western front.' Fortunately the 5th (Hunts) Battalion of the Northants Regiment suffered no casualties and managed to capture a German gramophone and 22 records! The first Huntingdonshire war fatality was 16-year-old Arthur Flack of Earith, who was killed off Norway in May 1940. He had been in the Navy since he was 14. In the same month Pilot Officer Norman Smith and Leading Aircraftman Stanley Maddox, both old boys of Huntingdon Grammar School, were reported missing in air operations. In June, wounded and exhausted soldiers began to arrive back in Huntingdon from Dunkirk. The Gem cinema was requisitioned for billeting the men evacuated from France. However, during the first year of the war just three men from Huntingdon itself were killed.

Just as they had during World War One, local newspapers celebrated families who had several sons serving in the forces. One such family lived at 15 Cowper Road. Mr and Mrs Chambers had four sons: John Charles (aged 37) had joined the 5th Northants, and had also served in the last war; Ernest Victor (32) was in the Suffolk Regiment; George Albert (24) and Joseph Kitchener (22) had both just joined up. Little more than a year later Joseph Chambers was in enemy hands. He was one of four men from Cowper Road who were prisoners of war. However, he wrote to his mother from his POW camp reassuring her that he was well, sending his best wishes to his friends, and asking her to take care of his fishing tackle!

Cowper Road. (The authors)

George Chambers spent four and a half years in the central Mediterranean, where he saw much action, but escaped injury.

The men of Cowper Road serve as a good cross section of the impact of war on a single street. By 1941 four mothers knew that their sons were in enemy hands. In March 1943 Sergeant Air Gunner Ronald William Gutteridge of 44 Cowper Road was killed on active service. Other families in Cowper Road had better news. Flight Sergeant Harold 'Monty' Watson, son of Mrs Lilley at number 22, was awarded the DFM in February 1944. One of his neighbours, T. Cooper who was serving in the Merchant Navy, was pictured in *The Hunts Post* when he met up with two other Huntingdon lads, H. Humphrey and R. Nicholson, in Malta. Another Cowper Road man, William Carter, was featured when he met up with three other Huntingdonshire boys in Italy. These stories would have been reflected in other streets throughout the town. For example, the family of Corporal Joe King, who was serving in the Royal Army Medical Corps, would have celebrated when their son and just one other comrade captured 200 Italians. There would have been very different feelings at Orchard House when he was later reported missing in north-west Europe.

'So vile and powerful a foe...'

Huntingdon was relatively unaffected by enemy action, but this did not mean that local officials did not take the situation seriously. There were constant appeals for volunteers, ARP wardens, fire watchers, auxiliary firemen, nurses and those to help care for evacuees. The Mayor of Huntingdon motivated local people to 'do their bit': 'never before has this country had to face so vile and powerful a foe. So revolting are these beasts that no infamy is too great for them... the callous machine-gunning of helpless Belgian civilians; the diabolical slaying of refugees on open roads; the bombing of hospitals.'

The fact that the headquarters of the Pathfinder Squadron, one of the most highly-trained elite forces of the RAF, whose job it was to locate and mark German targets for attack by bomber command, were in Castle Hill House from June 1943 made the town a possible target, but despite the heavy emphasis on maintaining the black out Huntingdon saw little in the way of enemy attack. Although 567 high explosive bombs and 4,468 incendiary bombs fell on the county between 1940 and 1943 there was little damage, and casualties were light. Enemy action accounted for only seven deaths and 18 injuries. The most serious incident in Huntingdon itself occurred on the night of 12 August 1941, when the Luftwaffe dropped 47 anti-personnel bombs on the town. Houses, shops and telephone wires were damaged, but there were no casualties. Unlike modern war reporting, none of these events were reported in the press. The only thing which was reported as falling from the sky over Huntingdon was a yellow dinghy which fell from a low flying RAF plane on to 'Waverlea' in Hartford Road, just as the house's owner, Mrs Clifton, was returning home.

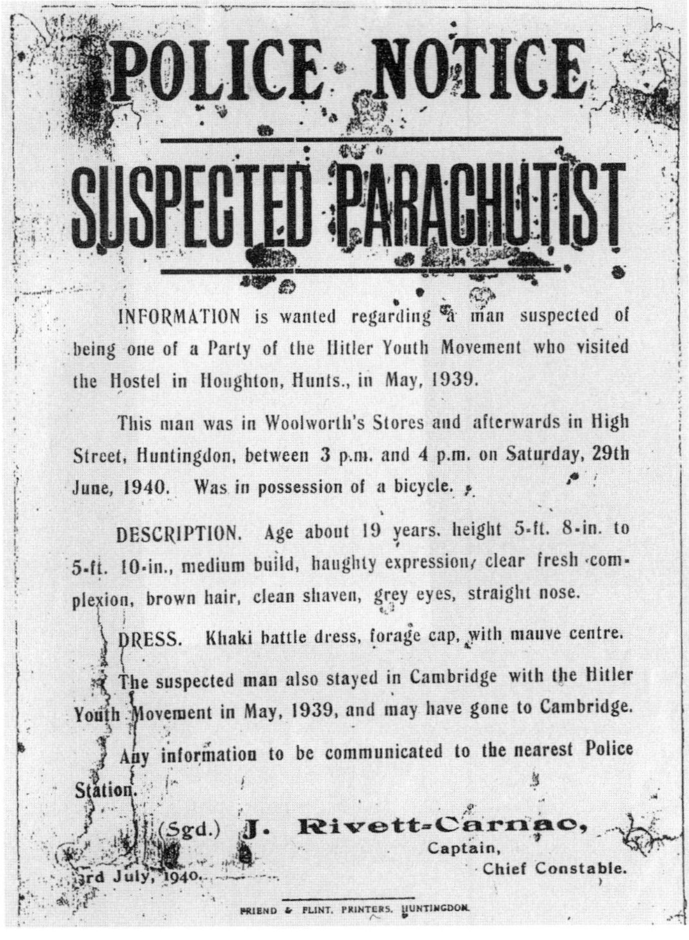

POLICE NOTICE

SUSPECTED PARACHUTIST

INFORMATION is wanted regarding a man suspected of being one of a Party of the Hitler Youth Movement who visited the Hostel in Houghton, Hunts., in May, 1939.

This man was in Woolworth's Stores and afterwards in High Street, Huntingdon, between 3 p.m. and 4 p.m. on Saturday, 29th June, 1940. Was in possession of a bicycle.

DESCRIPTION. Age about 19 years. height 5-ft. 8-in. to 5-ft. 10-in., medium build, haughty expression, clear fresh complexion, brown hair, clean shaven, grey eyes, straight nose.

DRESS. Khaki battle dress, forage cap, with mauve centre.

The suspected man also stayed in Cambridge with the Hitler Youth Movement in May, 1939, and may have gone to Cambridge.

Any information to be communicated to the nearest Police Station.

(Sgd.) J. Rivett-Carnac,
Captain,
Chief Constable.

3rd July, 1940.

FRIEND & FLINT, PRINTERS, HUNTINGDON.

Huntingdonshire Constabulary poster, 1940. (County Record Office Huntingdon: accession 172)

In fact, during the early days of the war more people were killed or injured by the black out than by the enemy. In December 1940 Mr E.W. Elphick was injured when he knocked his teeth out tripping over the low railing of the war memorial in Market Hill. Many people were killed or hurt on the unlit roads, too. Other accidents also took their toll. In August 1940 a soldier was killed fooling about with his rifle at Huntingdon Barracks, and several soldiers were drowned swimming in local rivers and gravel pits.

Local people would have been in no doubt, however, about the horrors of war. Hinchingbrooke House became a convalescent hospital, first for soldiers and then for civilian air raid casualties – a haven of peace for them, but a reminder for local people of what was happening elsewhere. The Red Cross nurses did an excellent job at Hinchingbrooke, according to Mr H.T. Baily of St Albans, who went there after being injured in an air raid on London in November 1940: 'I can truthfully say I

Hinchingbrooke Cottage. The Earl and Countess of Sandwich moved here when Hinchingbrooke House became a convalescent hospital. They never moved back into the house, but sold it along with the rest of the estate in 1962. Hinchingbrooke Cottage became the headquarters of Cambridgeshire Fire and Rescue Service. (The authors)

have never had better treatment in my life before. The staff were real Christians, always willing to help patients in whatever trouble they may have. The food was splendid and I shall never forget the four months I spent there.' Soldiers were to be found at Hinchingbrooke again in April 1944, followed by victims of the flying bombs. By the time it closed as a hospital in October 1945, 5,530 patients had been treated there.

There were constant reminders of the war all over the town – gun emplacements, concrete tank traps along Hartford Road and the prisoner of war camps set up along St Peter's Road and Stukeley Road – but the biggest impact of the war for most people would have been the introduction of rationing. After the experiences of World War One, the residents of Huntingdon must have expected shortages, and sure enough petrol rationing began on Friday 22 September 1939. *The Hunts Post* reported that people had filled up before rationing began and 'on Saturday there was not a gallon of petrol to be had in Huntingdon'. In February 1940 there was a serious coal shortage in Huntingdon and schools had to close due to lack of fuel. Men who delivered coal suddenly found themselves very popular. When one of Huntingdon's coalmen arrived in Brampton on his round he was greeted on the doorstep by a housewife 'whose joy knew no bounds – she hardly gave me time to put my bag down before giving me a kiss'.

Food rationing was soon in place too, and communal feeding centres and wartime canteens once again became a feature of Huntingdon's town centre. A former Territorial hut in St Mary's Street opened in November 1939 as a food and social centre for the troops. A cooking centre called the British Restaurant opened at the Trinity Schoolroom in October 1940, under the auspices of the Women's Voluntary Service (WVS): its purpose was to provide meals for evacuees and workers, but it was open to everyone. By December 1941 an average of 250 people were eating there each day, dining on such things as sausages, cabbage and potatoes followed by steamed pudding and custard. By 1943 the British Restaurant was serving 80,000 meals a year.

Gun emplacement on the railway bridge across Ermine Street. (County Record Office Huntingdon: 1096/109)

In October 1939 tractors were sent by the Ministry of Agriculture for the Hunts

War Agricultural Executive Committee, initially for ploughing up grassland. Instructions were also given that allotments and gardens should be cultivated to their fullest extent. By early November about 400 acres of extra land had been ploughed. As the war progressed, however, higher and higher agricultural targets were set. In January 1941, for instance, the Ministry of Agriculture asked the War Agricultural Executive Committee for an extra 3,000 acres of potatoes in the county. Lack of labour was a problem, but Major Proby, Chairman of the WAEC told the Minister that 'this county will do its damndest to complete the task'. The county was obviously doing something right, as later in the year US agriculturalists visited Huntingdon to inspect reclaimed land. Inspections were carried out to make sure gardens were properly cultivated. Five in Cowper Road were reported as being neglected, possibly because many of the men from Cowper Road were serving in the armed forces.

Over paid, over sexed and over here

The entry of the US into the war resulted in many American troops being stationed in or near Huntingdon. In 1942 a club was opened for the use of US forces stationed locally. The Freemasons offered the use of their headquarters The Priory for the purpose. The centre was run by the US Red Cross with the help of local volunteers and was the first one of its kind anywhere in England. During the first few weeks it was in operation men from 31 different US states had signed the visitor's book. A year later Sergeant Lauren Glosser summed up what the provision of such facilities meant to servicemen a long way from home. Under the heading 'A thousand thanks from a thousand Yanks', he wrote 'I dare say that there is no agreement between political heads of governments and no treaties written on paper, which would have had so much effect on Anglo-American relations as have the many kindnesses we have received in this club from our British friends.'

Anglo-American relations were cemented in the many marriages which took place. The first United States Air Force officer to marry a Huntingdon girl was Duncan Higgins, who married 22-year-old Helena Peacock in November 1943. From the summer of 1944 onwards, when the end of the war was in sight and it was apparent that the Americans would not be staying much longer, there was a rush of weddings: at St Mary's parish church between September 1944 and May 1945, for example, eight out of the 14 marriages involved American servicemen. There were also many liaisons that never reached marriage.

Priory House, situated next to Cromwell House, was used by US forces during the war. (County Record Office Huntingdon: WH2/177)

As well as the Americans, Czech soldiers were made welcome in Huntingdon too. Many of them were enter-

Left: *Members of the American Red Cross visit the George Hotel in the 1940s.* (County Record Office Huntingdon: accession 3521)

Right: *The American Red Cross delivering doughnuts to US forces in Huntingdon, 1940s.* (County Record Office Huntingdon: accession 3521)

tained in private homes over Christmas 1943. In September 1945, some of the Czech soldiers who had spent time in Huntingdon returned for short holidays with the friends they had made. Unfortunately, many had failed to find their relatives when they returned home to Czechoslovakia.

Contributing to the war effort

In July 1940, as Britain was threatened with air attack, Lord Beaverbrook appealed for aluminium to make Spitfires. Pots and pans were collected and sent to the

The Sebastopol Cannon, next to the County Hospital in George Street, was a trophy from the Crimean War. It was removed for salvage in 1942. (County Record Office Huntingdon: PH48/83)

county supply depot at Huntingdon. Within a week six hundredweight of aluminium had been collected. The Sebastopol cannon on Mill Common was removed and used for scrap metal. Iron railings were another target: they were to be reused, mainly for tanks. Enough iron for 440 tanks was collected in the eastern region by June 1942. As time went on, salvage drives were a regular feature and targets were generally exceeded. In November 1942, Godmanchester achieved the highest income for non-borough councils from salvage per head of population in England, while Huntingdon managed fourth place for borough councils in September the same year.

Boy Scouts collected so much waste paper for recycling that they had difficulty coping with all the paper. Scout HQ in St Germain Street, which was 35ft by 18ft, and 15ft high, was completely jammed with paper, right up to the ceiling. Woolworths lent the scouts a baler to bring some order to the chaos.

The main push by the government, however, was for war savings. People across England were encouraged to lend money by buying Government Savings Bonds or Certificates. An almost unbelievable amount of money was raised in this way through different campaigns in Huntingdonshire. In September 1940, a Spitfire Fund was launched. Within two months, the county had raised over £5,000, with Huntingdon itself contributing £1,089 17s 9d. In March 1941 War Weapons Week aimed to pay for 40 aircraft. An impressive programme of events, including a fly past by the RAF and a production of *Murder in the Cathedral* at St Mary's Church, was planned. A parade by the Home Guard and a display by the Royal Horse Artillery launched proceedings on Sunday. By Wednesday, Huntingdon and Godmanchester had raised £103,758; by the end of the week, three times the target amount had been raised (£676,933 for the county – £12 per head), with Huntingdon and Godmanchester achieving savings of £190,127. Lord Sandwich stated that everyone had done their bit: 'I think there is little doubt that the large majority of this figure... has been contributed by small sums from working people. This makes the success of the week even more satisfactory.'

A newspaper advertisement for War Weapons Week. (Hunts Post)

The Summer Savings Campaign was a more local affair, with each area setting its own target. For example, Huntingdon Central aimed for £250 for two machine guns and a Bren gun; North End WVS planned to raise £235 for two armour piercing shells and a rubber dinghy; Castle Hill WVS would buy a parachute and a heavy artillery shell with their £60; Godmanchester aimed to raise £300 for a light ambulance; even the Huntingdon branch of Woolworths had a target, £14 for two rifles.

Warship Week was held during March 1942, to fund HMS *Ramsey*. There were naval exhibitions in Huntingdon's Town Hall, parades, dances, musical evenings, a cookery demonstration and a gigantic darts tournament. The county raised £609,854 for the ship, almost £11 per head of the county's population: Ramsey, unsurprisingly, achieved the highest contribution with £15 per head, but Huntingdon itself raised a tremendous £157,571. Part of the reason why Huntingdon's response was so good may lie in the loss of the SS *Huntingdon* only a few weeks earlier. The SS *Huntingdon* had been built by the Federal Steam Company in 1922, but on 24 February 1942 she was torpedoed and sunk by a German U-boat in the North Atlantic – so perhaps Huntingdon's inhabitants were hoping HMS *Ramsey* would redress the balance.

The SS Huntingdon, *sunk by the German navy in 1942.* (County Record Office Huntingdon: MD5/17/4)

The following year's drive, launched in Huntingdon by King Peter of Yugoslavia, saw all its targets smashed, too. Huntingdon aimed to raise enough for ten Spitfires while St Ives aimed for three Wellington Bombers. The two towns were in competition to see who could raise the most after a bet between the two Mayors. St Ives won, and Huntingdon's Mayor L.G. Beardmore had to buy a new hat for Mr C. Harrison, Mayor of St Ives, as a result. Huntingdon's target during Salute the Soldier Week in 1944 was £50,000, to clothe and equip a base hospital. Bearing in mind how much people had already saved, the figure of £84,592 raised is extraordinary.

Just as they had during World War One, many local businesses, groups and individuals made a valuable contribution to the local war effort. Employees at the Huntingdon Hosiery Mill gave a concert, the highlight of which was a mock fight between 'Mr Chamberlain' and 'Herr Hitler' performed by two brothers, William and Richard Cumberland. There was standing room only at the concert, which raised £11 15s 6d. Huntingdon Grammar School put on plays for the War Charities Fund, and pupils were encouraged to save a penny a week for the same cause. The Red Cross held regular fêtes at Hinchingbrooke, usually drawing crowds of over 5,000. In 1941, 1,500 people paid 6d each to see the famous St Neots Quads playing in the little house on the Hinchingbrooke estate. Over £5,000 was raised by the Red Cross Fête Committee between 1942 and 1944.

The most outstanding personal contribution made by any individual was that of J.A. Fielden, a former High Sheriff of the county who once lived at Lawrence Court in Huntingdon but later moved to Holmewood Hall. By the time he died, aged 82, in November 1942 Fielden had donated around £800,000 during both world wars. During World War One he had donated enough to equip and maintain a hospital ship; during World War Two he paid for four Spitfires, one of which shot down four German aircraft. One of the Spitfires was named *Holmewood* in his honour. Fielden was a great admirer of the RAF and once said 'if I had sons, I would want to see them in the RAF. As it is, money is the only weapon an old man like me can fight with.' His weapon was a powerful one – £800,000 is the equivalent of £21 million today.

The Spotlights Concert Party performing Going Up *in Huntingdon in 1942.* (County Record Office Huntingdon: accession 1598)

Not everyone worked selflessly for the successful progress of the war. Petty crime was rife throughout the war years: the hospital collecting box was stolen by soldiers; a girl stole from the cash till at the US Red Cross Club; water was added to milk. William Nichols, a butcher of 57 High Street, was found guilty in May 1941 of selling sausages that contained 'too much' meat. He claimed ignorance of the new regulations regarding the content of sausages (they should contain only 30–40 percent meat), but as he was chairman of the Huntingdon Butchers Association, the court felt this was unlikely. With the words 'ignorance is no excuse' the judge fined him £23 15s for 80 offences.

One of the most common crimes was stealing petrol, often by siphoning it from military vehicles, or even from bombers parked on airfields. In October 1942 a petrol conspiracy centred on Murkett's garage was uncovered. Logbooks had been faked, and petrol was acquired and supplied without coupons. The forged logbooks were later burnt in a failed attempt to conceal the evidence of a 'long series of transactions dealing with enormous quantities of petrol in complete and absolute defiance of all the regulations'. The three Murkett brothers, Harry, Alfred and William, their sales manager William Kirby, and Albert Gill, a Godmanchester garage proprietor, received sentences ranging from two years to 10 months, plus fines. Several well-known residents were also implicated in the scandal, including the Deputy Mayor of Huntingdon, four police constables and Sir William Prescott, former High Sheriff of the county and member of Huntingdonshire County Council, who had received 93 gallons of petrol between November 1940 and June 1941. Sir William was fined £500 and, of course, his good name was tarnished, which the judge described as 'a shocking tragedy'.

Housing the evacuees

As early as January 1939 the British Government had been planning to evacuate more than a million children from London in the event of war. Huntingdon Borough Council began to survey potential accommodation, and at the end of August, as war seemed inevitable, detailed figures of what Huntingdon could expect

HUNTS. POST, THURSDAY, SEPTEMBER 7, 1939

CHILDREN INVADE HUNTINGDONSHIRE

Arrival of the first train load of evacuated children from London on Friday at Huntingdon North Station. In the centre is Mr. W. T. Carter (headmaster of Brampton School) with megaphone, directing the children where to go to receive rations before boarding the waiting buses to convey them to the villages.

Evacuees arriving in Huntingdon. (Hunts Post)

were published. There were to be 1,782 evacuees assigned to the town: 620 unaccompanied children and 62 teachers, with the remaining 1,100 made up of women with children under five and others.

Evacuees had already started to arrive in Huntingdon before war was declared. The first train arrived at 9.55am on Friday 1 September 1939 and carried girls from Highbury and Tollington Park. Mr W.T. Carter, headmaster of Brampton School, was in charge of operations at Huntingdon Station, and issued instructions through a large megaphone. Everyone was orderly and well behaved as they crossed the bridge and assembled on Mill Common. According to *The Hunts Post,* some children were so thrilled to be in a field that they danced and ran around. They carried with them pillowcases and haversacks containing a change of clothing, gymshoes and a day's supply of food. Each had three identity labels attached to them. The girls passed through a food tent, where they were given a tin of corned beef; a tin of unsweetened milk and one of sweetened milk, two packets of biscuits, and a quarter of a pound of chocolate. After drinking mugs of water the evacuated children boarded buses to be taken to various villages and towns throughout the county. Everything possible was done to ensure that families were not split up. A second train arrived at 10.45am, and another at 4.20pm. On Saturday and Sunday the expectant mothers and those with babies arrived.

More evacuees arrive in Huntingdon. (Hunts Post)

The evacuees came from Harringay, Hornsey, Tottenham, Tollington and Highbury Vale. It was estimated that 6,000 people arrived in Huntingdon between Friday and Sunday. Most were sent outside Huntingdon itself. Hinchingbrooke Park and Edward House were used to house London nursery schools. The clerk to the County Council, Mr B. Kelly, put his house at Mill Common at the disposal of the authorities. The Trinity schoolroom in Huntingdon was transformed into a social centre for evacuees.

In October 1939 about 400 school age children were moved back to Huntingdon from the villages, in order to keep their classes together. The old Grammar School was reopened to accommodate them. By January 1940 there were more than 500 evacuees in the town itself (rather fewer than the 1,782 who had been expected), comprising 426 unaccompanied school children, 30 unaccompanied pre-school children, 20 mothers, 31 teachers and four helpers.

This influx of people had a considerable effect on the small market town, and many residents were far from happy about it. Letters appeared in local newspapers complaining about the evacuees, who were accused of 'taking advantage' by begging for food and clothing when they had plenty of money. There were also complaints that the allocation of 8s 6d was not enough to feed a teenager (the allowance was 10s 6d per week for one child, or 8s 6d if there was more than one). It was claimed that local children were having their own education disrupted. Meal times were awkward as schools were working in shifts.

By February 1940 there were plans for Huntingdon to receive another 500 evacuees if London were bombed. Even the Borough Council now started to protest about housing them, claiming that there was no more room. Many of the larger houses in the town had already been requisitioned by the military so there was no spare capacity. Adverts were placed in local papers, urging residents to register to take evacuees, but there was little response. Huntingdon Borough Council sent out 1,500 letters with a form to be filled in by those willing to be placed on the register of those who would take refugees: only 65 people replied, 41 of whom already had evacuees living with them. Compulsion was the only alternative, and in May 1940, Walter Dunkley of Brampton became the first person to be fined for refusing to take an evacuee.

The evacuees themselves did not always make things easy for those looking after them. In December 1943 a pair of seven-year-old twins were said to be 'out of control' after they had stolen objects from the Roman Catholic Church, set fire to a lorry, stolen hand grenades, damaged the cricket pavilion in St Peter's Road and much more. They could not blame separation from their parents, both their mother and father were in Huntingdon too.

In 1942 the Borough Council constructed some new sandpits on Mill Common and in Hartford Road Recreation Ground, so that children were not robbed of the delights of a seaside holiday. (Hunts Post)

Women volunteers dig the foundations of new defence works around Huntingdon. (Hunts Post)

Yet there was much kindness towards the evacuees, too. Alderman and Mrs F. Clark gave over their house in Hartford Road to the evacuee family living with them, when the daughter of the family was married at St Mary's Church. On Christmas

Day 1940 about 140 evacuee mothers, children and old folk were entertained to lunch and tea at the communal feeding centre at Trinity Church.

The schoolchildren from London kept their own identity. The girls from Highbury Hill High School, for example, were taught by their own teachers and used the old Grammar School buildings. They put on school productions of their own, and had separate sports days. This did not mean that the children did not become involved with the local community, however. In October 1942 Highbury Hill girls were helping local schoolgirls with the fruit harvest. About 40 volunteers were leaving Huntingdon each day to work from 6.00 to 9.00pm on local farms. It was not until July 1944 that there were proposals to amalgamate Highbury Hill High School with Huntingdon Grammar as, by this time, only 59 pupils remained in Huntingdon.

The numbers of evacuees in Huntingdon were constantly changing. A lull in the bombing at the end of 1941 meant that 40 percent of the evacuees in Huntingdon had returned home, but it was more or less cancelled out by the inflow of unofficial evacuees, war workers and serving men's wives and families, many of whom were working locally. The town's population, which normally numbered 4,600, stood at 6,220 in November 1941. Attacks by flying bombs in London meant that another influx of evacuees arrived in July 1944. Hartford School had to accommodate 50 evacuee pupils. In the end half-time schooling had to be introduced in local schools, locals having lessons in the morning, evacuees in the afternoon.

In July 1945 the last few pupils of Highbury Hill finally returned to London. Many, of course, had no homes to return to. They all gathered in the old Grammar School to say goodbye. Huntingdon Grammar School was presented with a silver cup to commemorate the happy relations between the two schools for the past six years. Many girls were invited back to Huntingdon for holidays.

Peace at last

Corporal Frederick Wright of the Royal Corps of Signals arrived home at 58 Cowper Road in August 1944 as the first liberated prisoner of war to return to Huntingdon. Despite five years as a prisoner of the Nazis he was still disappointed with the town on his arrival, commenting that 'I'm sorry to say that I think Huntingdon could still do a lot more for the services – there is no more entertainment now than there was when I left.' Corporal Wright had a sister in the ATS and a brother in the army. Victor Darnell, son of Mrs Arnold of 42 Cowper Road, had also been a prisoner for five years, being released in March 1945. Another Cowper Road resident, Mrs Verral of number 35, learned that her son, Private Flisher, had been liberated by the American 9th Army in May. He had been captured at Oudenarde in May 1940, been set to work on a farm, then transferred to Marionberg and elsewhere. Typical of many returning POWs, he thanked the Red Cross 'from the bottom of my heart' for the parcels which had kept them going. As prisoners of war began to be released, and the threat of enemy attack receded,

Huntingdon started to relax and look forward to the peace. Air Defence Cadets at Huntingdon Grammar no longer had to act as aircraft spotters on the school roof, and the Home Guard was officially 'stood down' on 3 December 1944. About 700 members of the Home Guard, many of them veterans of World War One, paraded through Huntingdon as they were officially relieved of their duties. They were commended by their commanding officer, Lieutenant Colonel W.E. Wilson: 'you have helped to turn defeat into the coming complete victory; you have done your duty honourably and well'. As General Hayes said, speaking at Hemingford Park, 'these are the men who would have fought nobly and to the death if Hitler's men had invaded our land'.

Farewell to the Home Guard, 1944. (Hunts Post)

Hunts Post

THE COUNTY PAPER FOR HUNTINGDONSHIRE

THURSDAY, DECEMBER 7, 1944

THE PEOPLE'S ARMY MARCHES FOR THE LAST TIME

Home Guard Gets Final "Dismiss"

H.G. STAND DOWN. — Two photos taken at the 2nd Battn. parade at Huntingdon on Sunday. Left: One of the contingents leaving the Old

Cafeterias For Hunts?

The real celebrations began in May 1945 following the German surrender. Even then there was a realisation of the seriousness of the moment. According to *The Hunts Post*, 'uppermost in the thoughts of everyone was a sober feeling of thankfulness that the ordeal which has lasted five and a half years was over at last, while the knowledge that the Far East enemy has still to be brought to her knees acted as a further influence checking and tendency to "Mafekinging". None the less there was naturally intense jubilation throughout the county.' Huntingdon was ablaze with flags, most shops, offices and factories were closed for two days, and a speech by Churchill was relayed to a large crowd in Market Hill. The square was floodlit, and there was dancing until late. However, according to *The Hunts Post* 'great offence was given to many people at Huntingdon by the action of a young WAAF who climbed on to the figure of the soldier forming the town's fine war memorial and placed a cigarette between the lips.'

VE Day celebrations in Huntingdon, May 1945. (Huntingdon Library)

Cowper Road was one of many streets to hold a party, organised by Mrs Craghill, Mrs Johnson and Mrs Stephenson. There was a 'delicious spread' laid on for over a hundred children, followed by sports such as egg and spoon and tug of war. Each

VJ Day celebrations, August 1945. (Huntingdon Library)

child was presented with a 3d piece. Helpers at the event included two former prisoners of war from Cowper Road, Privates Flisher and Jesse Clifton.

In June demobbed soldiers began to arrive home. The first Huntingdonian to be demobbed was Wireman W.T. Hayward of 34 Cowper Road. He arrived home in

A peace parade on Mill Common, 1946. (County Record Office Huntingdon: PH100A/3)

the early hours of Saturday morning, 23 June, after serving four and a half years in the Royal Navy.

VJ Day brought further celebrations in the town. There was a comic cricket match where a council XI, dressed in their civic robes, took on a ladies XI – the ladies won. Eight hundred children were entertained to tea at the American Red Cross Hostel. Three thousand people attended a huge bonfire on the Hartford Road playing fields. Figures of Hitler and Hirohito were strung across St Germain Street, while Cowper Road held another street party. Most pubs had by this time run out of beer. 'Just after 1am the dancing stopped. This was earlier than the previous night, yet it was quite clear that this was not through lack of interest, but through sheer physical exhaustion.'

CHAPTER 8

'We want this town to grow': Post-war Huntingdon

EVEN BEFORE the end of the war, councillors in Huntingdon were discussing the need for post-war development. Houses were badly needed for returning servicemen and their families, but progress was painfully slow. Fourteen new houses were due to be built at Ambury Hill, but there were many delays, mainly due to a shortage of bricklayers. Those waiting for accommodation were understandably frustrated, particularly when they could see so much government-owned land standing idle. In September 1946, their patience ran out. Mr and Mrs Smith and Mr and Mrs Gilks, with their six children, became Huntingdon's first squatters when they took over the empty POW camp in Stukeley Road. The families had previously been living in one bedroom. Three more families

An aerial photograph showing the World War Two huts behind Castle Hill House, occupied unofficially by people on the housing list in 1947. (Peterborough Citizen and Advertiser)

joined them during the following week. They were sharing a kitchen and had no electric light, but were, nevertheless, delighted with their new accommodation.

The promised houses at Ambury Rise were still only partly built. To ease the situation, the council began to erect 'prefabs' in Priory Lane. Eighteen had been completed by the following February: in fact 16 had already been occupied by squatters, standing up well to one of the coldest winters for 50 years. It was not enough, though, and more squatters moved in, this time into huts behind Castle Hill House. The new 'tenants' included one of Cowper Road's former POWs, Mr C. Foster. By May 1947 12 long-awaited houses had been completed; there were over 300 applicants for them. The first lucky family to move in were Mr and Mrs Dean, both lifelong Huntingdonians, and he a former POW. Mr and Mrs Tanner, who also moved in, had been waiting for a house since 1935. Obviously there were a lot of disappointed families. The next Borough Council meeting in June was the scene of strong protests. A petition with 120 names was handed in protesting about the situation: 'we the undersigned, view with disgust the fact that the present system of allocating Council Houses is, in our opinion, grossly unfair... we DEMAND to know why it is that families with no homes at all have had their applications ignored.'

It made no difference. Progress was slow, and the planned developments allowed for only 34 more families to be accommodated during 1947, with 40 more in 1948 and 1949. The building delays at Ambury Hill were so bad that the Ministry of Works was forced to investigate the problem in June 1948. To make matters worse, in November 1947 the squatters at Castle Hill House were given notice to quit by the Government, who wanted to use the buildings for offices. On appeal, the judge gave them until January to move out. The Borough Council claimed that it was 'helpless' to provide them with alternative accommodation. The Castle Hill squatters were eventually rehoused in WAAF accommodation at Alconbury.

The second phase of house building in American Lane faced just as many problems as the Ambury development. The design specifications had to be reduced when all the tenders came in at well over the £1,336 allowed by the Ministry. Shortages of wood meant that the council considered copper roofs; shortages of concrete led to yet more delays. It was not until August 1950 that the first lot of 31 houses (with tiled roofs in the end) was completed in American Lane.

Huntingdon was in such a bad way that even developments like the new bus station did not run smoothly. The concrete, which was supposed to be six inches thick, broke under the second bus to drive over it. In fact it was only two inches thick. The concrete had obviously been diverted elsewhere! Six months later complaints were received that there was no fire in the waiting room and that the toilets were in a disgusting condition.

Rationing continued through 1948, and the elderly and needy residents of Huntingdon were grateful to the people of their sister town, Huntingdon in Quebec, for the one and a half tons of food which they sent over. The consignment included large quantities of lard, tea, dried fruit, tinned meat and fish, butter, soup, jam and jelly.

One of the recipients, Mrs Frank Goods of Ermine Street, told a *Hunts Post* reporter that she would hurry home with her allocation and enjoy a bread and dripping supper.

On the social side, though, things might be said to be improving. The first meeting at the new greyhound stadium, which opened on Sapley Lane, was held on 20 September 1947. In October, a new youth centre opened – a converted Nissen hut in Castle Hill grounds, formerly used as the operations room of RAF Pathfinder Force. Evening classes were booming, but people obviously had less time for sports. The Huntingdon Golf Club, which had been in operation for 57 years, closed in May 1947 due to dwindling membership.

'Not a manufacturing town'

In his directory of 1839 Pigot said that Huntingdon 'is not a manufacturing town', and indeed until the 1950s most of the industry in Huntingdon was based on processing, servicing, or making machinery for the agriculture of the surrounding area. Ruston's, for example, had started out as an ironmongers' shop in the High Street, but when farms increasingly became mechanised the firm expanded into the manufacture of agricultural machinery. In 1950 Ruston's took over the Wood and Ingram site in St Germain Street and built a factory, which by 1959 was employing 70 people. The Chivers company, which moved into the former Windover factory in Brampton Road in 1930, was canning vegetables grown locally, including peas, broad beans, carrots, beetroot and spinach. The company flourished: many new buildings were added and a former flour mill in Godmanchester was needed for extra warehouse space. The factory had an ideal location near the railway, to which it had direct access via a siding. Chivers later diversified into jam making, and by 1959 the company employed around 500 people in Huntingdon, making it the largest cannery of its kind in the country. Chivers were later taken over by Batchelor foods, and the factory was closed in 1966.

Rustons Engineering Co. Ltd's premises in St Germain Street. This building was demolished in 1992. (County Record Office Huntingdon: accession 3312)

Chivers factory staff, photographed during the 1940s or 1950s. (County Record Office Huntingdon: accession 4970)

Other firms in Huntingdon were those which had been able to change with the times. Murkett Brothers, which had been operating as a cycle and motorcycle manufacturer since the 1890s, kept up with new developments and began to sell cars too. The adaptability of the firm was shown during the war years when petrol rationing made the car business less profitable, at which point Murketts then began to deal in sports goods. By 1950 Murkett Brothers were operating from large premises on the High Street, the former Fountain Hotel.

Interior of a bicycle workshop, possibly Murketts. (County Record Office Huntingdon: WH2/169)

Before World War One Windovers was the only large firm in Huntingdon. The carriage works at the end of George Street was famous throughout the country, and the company made carriages for royalty. In 1899 Charles Windover set up George Maddox in business making cars and carriages. He was soon employing about 100 men, but the factory was destroyed by fire in 1924. The site in Hartford Road later became a large garage, Maddox and Kirby.

Industries tended to be located in the town centre, or near the railway like Chivers and the Huntingdon Hosiery Mill. The area around Handcroft Lane and Ferrars Road was one of the early industrial areas of the town and the notable exception to the agricultural connection. Edison Bell had a factory there making gramophones and gramophone records. There was great excitement in the town when the factory burned to the ground in 1928. It was, according to the *Hunts Post*, 'perhaps the greatest blaze Huntingdon has seen'. Edison Bell closed down in 1930. It was replaced by Silent Channel who bought the factory in 1936 and began

Windovers factory in George Street, photographed before it was destroyed by fire in 1924. Chivers later took over the site. (County Record Office Huntingdon: WH3/2626)

Mr R.V. Howes in his shoe repair factory in Queen's Head Passage, 1950. (County Record Office Huntingdon: PH48/169/2)

production there in 1937. A sister company, the Huntingdon Rubber Company, was set up in the original factory in 1953. Silent Channel moved into a new purpose-built factory in 1955, by which time they had 250 employees. Rubber products were made on the site for the next half century despite several changes of name, to Standard Products and then to Cooper Standard, and the loss of 350 jobs in 1999.

There was some diversification of industry during World War Two when several companies moved to the relative safety of Huntingdon after being bombed in London. The Oriental Confectionery Manufacturers Ltd arrived in St Germain Street in 1941 after damage to their London premises. They made Turkish Delight, marshmallow and fudge, and exported to the US, New Zealand and the West Indies, as well as to some Mediterranean countries. Another wartime arrival was the Acoustical Manufacturing Company Ltd, later the maker of the famous Quad brand of hifi equipment. Originally located in Ermine Street, the factory moved to St Peter's Hill in 1950.

The industries of Huntingdon played a large part in the war, often working in secret on projects which only came to light after the war. The Acoustical Manufacturing Company Ltd began making parts for the radios that were dropped by the RAF to Resistance fighters behind enemy lines. They were also turning out about 2,000 components per week for tank radios. P. & H. Engineering Ltd was set up in Hartford Road by four businessmen as a light engineering business. It was soon manufacturing incendiary bombs and flare casings. After Dunkirk, over 200,000 of P. & H.'s incendiary bombs were dispatched against the enemy. Chivers developed the first dehydration plant in England at Huntingdon, which was working almost continuously day and night after 1943. Workers at Silent Channel were

The entrance to Standard Products, formerly Silent Channel. This photograph was taken when the building was being offered for sale by Ekins estate agents. The building was demolished during the 1980s. (County Record Office Huntingdon: accession 4865)

also working six days and nights a week to make special compound rubber for use in ships' degaussing cables to combat magnetic mines. Army motor vehicle tyres, special rubber piping to enable vehicles to drive through water and rubber accessories for ARP helmets were also in production in Huntingdon. Volunteers at Huntingdon Hosiery Mill assembled gas masks at the start of the war, before turning their attention to socks for the army. According to *The Hunts Post*, 'socks from Huntingdon were soon on the march in every theatre of war'. Six and a half million pairs of socks left the Huntingdon factory during the war.

While Huntingdon's workers, many of whom were of course women, were pulling out all the stops for the war effort, local councillors were worrying about Government proposals for the dispersal of industry after the war. They were reluctant to see the rural, agricultural nature of Huntingdon's industry changing. After the war building restrictions were lifted, but it was not until the 1950s that new factories were built, mainly by existing companies within the town. Part of the problem was the lack of available land, much of which had been requisitioned by the Government during the war. Stukeley Road and Redwongs Way were earmarked for industrial development, but they were still in Government hands, a fact bemoaned by Councillor Ruston in 1946 when he said 'we want this town to grow – not to stagnate, but there is no likelihood of it growing while these various pieces of land are held by the Ministries, and in most cases empty'.

The 1950s

The Festival of Britain was supposed to be a tonic to the nation, but a subcommittee set up in Huntingdon to organise the events reported a complete lack of interest in the area. Nevertheless a Merrie England pageant was organised at Hinchingbrooke, the Borough Charters were put on display (again), All Saints Church was floodlit and street teas and dancing were organised.

Two years later Huntingdon had cause to unfurl its flags again to celebrate the Coronation of Elizabeth II. A Coronation pageant was specially written by the well-known Hilton author David Garnett and Revd Bagley. It consisted of eight episodes depicting scenes from history, and a grand finale. The pageant involved over 500 performers, musicians and helpers. It opened on 25 June and there were three performances, attended by a rather disappointing 1,151 people. Huntingdon saw six days of celebrations, the usual round of fancy dress parades, sports, dancing on Market Hill, and, of course, a display of the Borough archives. Unfortunately, many events were marred by rain and a blustery north wind.

These frivolities did not hide the fact that life in Huntingdon during the 1950s was not improving. Increasing demand for water and electricity meant that supply could not meet demand. People were asked to keep use of electricity to a minimum, but nonetheless Huntingdon faced cuts in supply on Mondays. During summer months even the new water tower on Views Common could not cope with demand. Health services were in no better state: an extension to facilities at the isolation

The Grand cinema, following the fire of 1954. (County Record Office Huntingdon: PH48/31)

hospital was put on hold due to a shortage of staff, while at the County Hospital there were 300 on the waiting list, and the children's ward had to be closed in December 1953 due to lack of staff. Things had not improved at the bus station either: complaints about the lack of lighting there were being made in 1958.

There was, however, plenty of entertainment available for the people of Huntingdon. The town had two cinemas (the Gem had closed in 1922 but had been replaced by the Hippodrome in 1934) and events were often staged at the Town Hall. The Grand Cinema, converted from the former Corn Exchange in 1912, was located at the back of Murkett's premises in the Market Square. In March 1954, however, disaster struck. Mr and Mrs William Murkett and their daughter Sheila woke at around 4am to find their bedrooms full of smoke. The Grand Cinema was well alight, and, as the fire brigade arrived, flames leapt into the air and the roof fell in. Firefighters from Huntingdon, St Ives and St Neots battled against the blaze, using water from the river at Portholme, but by morning the building was gutted.

The Huntingdon branch library opened in Gazeley House in December 1954. It had 1,679 members and was issuing 2,200 books per week. The merging of the Huntingdon fiction library, set up in the old Grammar School in 1952, with the headquarters library was highly successful. Huntingdon also boasted a new school. St Peter's School, the new secondary modern, opened on 12 September 1957 with 620 pupils from Huntingdon and the surrounding villages.

Huntingdon Branch Library in Gazeley House. (Huntingdon Library)

Progress on most fronts though was slow. The planned memorial hall to commemorate the fallen of World War Two was never built and the site earmarked for it in Nursery Road was abandoned. It was decided instead to convert the Literary Institute in the High Street, and this building was purchased in May 1956 for £3,000. By 1958 the fund stood at only £6,850, less than half the £15,000 needed, and work was not finally completed until January 1960, 15 years after the fund had been launched in July 1945. The Memorial Hall Committee had met exactly 100 times.

Huntingdon Swimming Club, founded in 1958, was unable to function during winter as there was still no heated pool. The Council was unable to provide a swimming pool and launched a swimming pool appeal, which

Bushey Close swimming pool. (Huntingdon Library)

had raised £1,500 by 1957. Money from the carnival, regular bingo sessions and other sources was relied on to provide the amenity, but by July 1959 only £4,000 was in the fund. The cost of a six-lane pool, 14 by 37 yards, had by now risen to £12,500. The swimming pool saga was typical of the slow progress in achieving anything in Huntingdon. Plans were made and meetings held, but by 1963 nothing had been achieved. In fact it was then decided that the pool should be located, not in Hartford Road as had been envisaged all along, but on the new Oxmoor estate. Construction was further delayed when builders working on the Technical College deposited heaps of soil on the proposed swimming pool site. Even when construction finally began in September 1964, the pool would take 50 weeks to complete, and its cost had risen to £51,000. The 150 members of Huntingdon Swimming Club had to travel to St Neots and Cambridge to swim. Finally, in September 1965, the pool was due to be handed over by the contractors to be filled by the fire brigade. Inevitably, things went wrong. Under the headline 'Pool a Swamp', *The Hunts Post* reported that the pool would not open after all. Councillor Turek said that the pool was 'an undescribable sea of mud'; the men's cubicles were not finished and the filtration plant was not working. Finally, nine years after the swimming pool appeal had been launched, Huntingdon's swimming pool opened in Bushey Close on 5 May 1966. The pool was 55 by 42 yards in size: the final cost was £65,000. The appeal fund had raised just £9,500. Despite the fact that the pool was unheated and the water temperature was only 57°F, 2,525 members of the public paid to use it in the first 10 days. The Olympic swimmer, Jackie Enfield, performed the official opening in June.

Clearly Huntingdon Borough Council was struggling to improve the social and economic life of the town. They did not have the resources to make large scale changes or improvements. The only way forward seemed to be to look for help from outside.

The opening times of the new swimming pool in Bushey Close. The printers misspelled the pool's name on the poster. (County Record Office Huntingdon: accession 3479)

HUNTINGDON & GODMANCHESTER BOROUGH COUNCIL

BUSHY CLOSE SWIMMING POOL

E. A. BLADES, Superintendent — Phone Huntingdon 4713

COMMENCING 3rd APRIL 1969, THE POOL WILL BE OPEN TO THE PUBLIC AT THE FOLLOWING TIMES

DURING SCHOOL TERM		DURING SCHOOL HOLIDAYS	
MONDAY	12.45 p.m. to 2.00 p.m. 4.15 p.m. to 8.30 p.m.	MONDAY – WEDNESDAY – THURSDAY & FRIDAY	10.00 a.m. to 12.00 noon 1.00 p.m. to 5.00 p.m. 6.00 p.m. to 8.30 p.m.
TUESDAY	12.45 p.m. to 2.00 p.m.	TUESDAY	10.00 a.m. to 12.00 noon 1.00 p.m. to 6.00 p.m.
WEDNESDAY	12.45 p.m. to 5.00 p.m. 6.00 p.m. to 8.30 p.m.	SATURDAY AND SUNDAY	10.00 p.m. (AM) to 1.00 p.m. 2.00 p.m. to 6.00 p.m.
THURSDAY	12.45 p.m. to 2.00 p.m. 4.15 p.m. to 8.30 p.m.		
FRIDAY	12.45 p.m. to 2.00 p.m. 4.15 p.m. to 8.30 p.m.		
SATURDAY	10.00 a.m. to 1.00 p.m. 2.00 p.m. to 6.00 p.m.		
SUNDAY	10.00 a.m. to 1.00 p.m. 2.00 p.m. to 6.00 p.m.		

LAST ADMISSION 45 MINUTES BEFORE THE ABOVE CLOSING TIMES

The evening closing times will vary during the early and latter part of the season
Persons under 14 years of age may be excluded from the pool one hour before the evening closing time unless accompanied by a responsible adult

ADMISSION CHARGES PER SESSION
Adult Bather 1/6 Spectator 1/-
Junior Bather 9d. Spectator 6d.
A JUNIOR IS A PERSON NOT HAVING ATTAINED THE AGE OF 16 ON APRIL 3RD 1969

Block Ticket - Child 12 for 7/6
Adult 12 for 15/-
Season Tickets for Juniors only. £1

CHAPTER 9

'A desirable conception of town planning': The Oxmoor Development

THE TOWN Development Act of 1952 was passed with the object of encouraging the development of county districts for the relief of congestion and over-population of the larger cities, notably London. It had two aims: to ease congestion in towns so that the quality of life for people living in 'difficult conditions' would be improved, and to infuse new life and vigour into static or declining country towns. It was obviously the second of these aims which appealed to Huntingdon Borough Council. Many towns near London were unwilling to take

Aerial view of Huntingdon taken before the town expansion began in the 1950s. (Peterborough Citizen and Advertiser)

part in the scheme, but small East Anglian towns such as Huntingdon, Haverhill and Thetford were anxious to reverse the decline of earlier years by receiving new industry and population, and to provide improved services of all kinds. Most of the public services in Huntingdon were, by this time, in an obsolete condition.

Huntingdon, St Neots, St Ives and Fletton were all under consideration for development, but not everyone was in favour. In January 1953, Alderman Clayton voiced the thoughts of many when he said 'I am a native of the County and we have four very nice countryside towns. I do not want to see them spoiled by Londoners.'

However, Huntingdon Borough Council applied for such a development, and by December 1955 London County Council had drawn up detailed plans to build 1,000 new houses in Huntingdon at a density of not less than 10 houses to each acre. On 12 April 1957 the Minister of Housing and Local Government confirmed that the new development could go ahead.

Huntingdon could not easily expand to the south or west so it was decided that land to the east, beyond Newtown and into Hartford, would be used for the 'overspill' estate. The name Oxmoor came from Oxmire Lane, a narrow muddy lane which gave access to the fields which would be developed.

The draft scheme was in place by 1957. A total of 184 acres of land would be purchased by the Borough Council, upon which 1,150 houses would be built, costing between £1,700 and £2,050 each. The rent would be £2 per week. Eighty percent of these houses would have garages. There would be an additional 50 acres for industrial development. The whole cost of the scheme would be £3 million.

Land was subject to compulsory purchase orders, which became the subject of a public enquiry. In March 1958 London County Council threatened to withdraw if the compulsory purchase of land in St Peter's Road, intended for industrial development, did not go ahead. Mr and Mrs Clifton and Mr Jakes, owners of some of the land, were reluctant to sell as they were unlikely to get its full market value. Once the report of the inquiry was published in September 1958 Mr Clifton, who owned Orchard Bungalow and 17½ acres of land, said that 'I cannot possibly buy similar premises and similar land for the money I shall get. It can't be done... I'm too young to retire and after all this I feel too old to start again. I don't know what I shall do.' There were additional complications because some of the land was common land.

Land acquired in St Peters Road for industrial development. (County Record Office Huntingdon: 1096/47)

There was a strong advertising campaign in both London and Huntingdon to encourage firms to move out of London, and to win over the support of the locals. Councillor Fiske, Chairman of the LCC Housing Committee, opened an exhibition on the development in Huntingdon Town Hall in May 1959. He said that the integration of the overspill population with Huntingdon people was vital: 'there should not be Londoners in exile'. Mr Ashpole, Borough Estate Officer, echoed these thoughts, urging local people to be welcoming. 'If such a thing does not happen,' he warned, 'you will find that the new residents will form a community of their own

Houses being built on Oxmoor Lane. (County Record Office Huntingdon: 1096/64)

and live apart from the town.' There was already animosity, however, when the building contracts were deemed too large for local firms and went to outsiders.

Work was due to start on 6 March 1960 but did not get underway until 28 June 1960. The contractors for the first phase were named as Johnson and Bailey Ltd. The first 184 houses and 36 flats were to be completed by the end of 1961, while the whole scheme of 1,150 houses was due for completion in 1965.

The design of the new estate was based on the layout of the American town of Radburn in New Jersey. Radburn had been planned in the 1920s according to a strict set of planning principles, the core philosophy behind which was to separate pedestrians from vehicles. Housing areas were arranged around large public greens, and were separated from each other by main roads; footpaths crossed the roads by means of bridges, walkways or subways. It was said to be 'a logical, convenient and desirable conception of town planning. Industry is grouped together away from the residential areas, and scheme takes account of the fact that pedestrians (and particularly children) can no longer be left to mingle with modern traffic.' The only concern at this stage was that the strip of common land between the estate and the town would form a barrier. It was hoped that the fact people would be mixing at work in the factories would overcome this problem. In March 1960 it was announced that the Vitaulic Company Ltd, a subsidiary of Stewarts and Lloyds Ltd, would be the first to move to Huntingdon from London, and would employ around 200 people.

At the same time the Council was making ambitious plans for the centre of Huntingdon. There was to be a pedestrian precinct of 40 shops built on the site of the Chequer Inn and the old brewery, which had been demolished earlier in the year. Bricks from the brewery chimney had been saved, and would be used in the new scheme. This would include a central square featuring terraces, steps, an ornamental pond and flowering shrubs. Queens Head Passage would also be developed with 30 shops, forming a link between the bus station and the town. The disused St Benedict's churchyard would be paved to make more space. (This development would be finally completed in 1981.) Land to the south-east of the proposed link road between George Street and Brookside would be set aside for a new post office, cinema and banks rather than for retail use. Plans even included suggestions for a helicopter station.

On 11 March 1961, the first families from London moved in. Numbers one and three Elm Close were the first houses to be completed. Mr Albert Knight, his wife

Suffolk House in Mayfield Road. (The authors)

Sylvia and two sons Clifford (14) and Martin (8) moved from a maisonette in Brixton. Mr Knight, a mould turner at Vitaulic, would continue to work in the factory at Elstree until the new factory opened in Huntingdon. They were welcomed by the local dignitaries, and the scheme as a whole was officially opened by Dame Evelyn Sharp, Permanent Secretary to the Ministry of Housing and Local Government. As the months went by further groups of Londoners visited Huntingdon to look at the new development. They would be shown the houses being built, and then entertained to tea in the Commemoration Hall where Mr Ashpole would answer their questions.

There were other momentous changes in Huntingdon's history occurring at this time. From 1 April 1961 the two boroughs of Huntingdon and Godmanchester became one, an arrangement which would last until April 1984 when they split to form two separate town councils (borough status having been lost in 1974).

By August 1961 the first factory, Vitaulic Ltd, was ready to go into production. Initially Vitaulic had only 50 employees, including some local women who had previously been working at the Chivers factory in the town, which was due for closure. The CRS factory was completed in October, and needed 40 workers, but no houses were ready, and none were expected to be ready until December. In the event, after 58 days lost to rain, and supply difficulties, these houses were not completed until July 1962. Some people were moving into unfinished houses. Only 97 houses had been occupied by the end of September. Mud was a problem, and the site was likened to a battlefield.

Marshall's Brewery, photographed in 1908. The brewery was demolished in 1960, and Chequers Court was built on its site. Bricks from the chimney were reused in the new buildings. (County Record Office Huntingdon: WH3/2317)

Oxmoor being built, April 1966. (County Record Office Huntingdon: PH48/14/4. Reproduced by permission of Simmons Aerofilm Ltd)

Things were progressing in the town centre, however. The first shop in the brewery development, Green and Wright's wine shop, opened in October 1961, selling Moet and Chandon champagne at 26s a bottle for anyone who wanted to celebrate. Mrs Elsie Pink, Mayor of the new joint Borough, laid an inscribed stone in the pavement at the entrance to the precinct. A further three shops were almost ready in the development aimed at giving Huntingdon 'a modern centre as befits a modern or overspill town'. In February 1962 a new clinic opened in Nursery Road, replacing services run from buildings in the grounds of the old Grammar School and Castle Hill House. For the first time, all the County Council healthcare services were together under one roof in a purpose-built clinic. Huntingdon's first supermarket, the *Home and Colonial*, was opened by the Mayor on 4 December 1962. In July 1963 Huntingdon's first launderette also opened in the new

The Home and Colonial, Huntingdon's first supermarket, part of the new Chequers Court development. (County Record Office Huntingdon: 1096/12)

The High Street, photographed before the changes which took place in the 1960s. The brewery in the foreground was demolished to make way for Chequers Court, while Trinity Church, in the background, was knocked down when its tower became unsafe. The church was replaced by a Tesco supermarket. A new Trinity Church was dedicated on the Oxmoor in 1968. (Huntingdon Library)

Tesco supermarket, built on the former High Street site of Trinity Church. (County Record Office Huntingdon: accession 3312)

precinct. By April 1966 a new Tesco supermarket was even offering late-night shopping.

On 9 May 1962 there was a second civic ceremony on the Oxmoor. This time Mr Henry Brooke, Chief Secretary to the Treasury and Paymaster General, former Minister of Housing and Local Government, performed the official opening, with a golden key, of Vitaulic's factory. Three months later 140 London employees of Horatio Myers Ltd, bedding manufacturers, who had volunteered to staff the new Huntingdon factory, visited the site of the new factory and the new houses being built. The Myers factory went into production on 27 May 1963. All 80 of its workforce came from London and as the factory expanded, more skilled labour was brought in from Vauxhall.

Soon, however, the Oxmoor dream started to go wrong. The development of housing and industry on the new estate was continuing, but there was little progress in the development of services to go with it. The new Oxmoor Estate Community Centre, opened by the mayor on 17 April 1963, was only a

Myers factory in St Peters Road. Myers began production in May 1963. (The authors)

'prefab'. After six years the estate still had no proper play areas. Older children had nothing to do either. Mr Barnett, who lived above the tobacconist shop in Mayfield Road, complained that 'they play with home-made go-karts and in racing try to get as near to the shop windows as possible. They play with footballs which sometimes hit the windows and race on cycles in and around supporting pillars, immediately in front of the shops. Groups of children run up and down the stairs and often have brick battles while clambering on the scaffolding of a new public house'. The scaffolding would disappear once the Lord Protector pub had been opened in April 1966 by Maurice Ashley, chairman of the Cromwell Association. From December 1965 the new Youth Centre in Sallowbush Road offered a variety of activities such as snooker, judo, weightlifting and dancing on five nights a week; but in general things did not improve much.

Unlike London there was very little public transport, and many former Londoners felt isolated enough to abandon Oxmoor. Five years after they moved in, one of the first families to relocate to Huntingdon, Mr and Mrs Hastings from 3 Elm Close, decided to emigrate to Australia. Huntingdon was still the same 'stick in the mud town' they had moved to: hospitals and services had not improved and the promised shops and playing fields had not materialised. It would be the end of 1967 before the first steps towards creating an adventure playground near Moorhouse Drive would be taken. A meeting of the Huntingdon Expansion Community Association held in November 1966 complained about low wages, employment shortages, lack of medical, entertainment and shopping facilities. It was claimed that 100–150 people would return to London if they had the opportunity. There was no doctor or post office on the estate and the schools were overcrowded. Mr J.H. Donald who had moved from White City described the Oxmoor estate as 'dead from the ankles up', despite the fact that the Lord Protector pub regularly held events such as discos and live bands.

Top: *Radio One DJ Johnny Walker visiting the Lord Protector pub, 1972.* (Hunts Post) *and* bottom : *Typical houses on the Oxmoor.* (The authors)

Unfortunately, Oxmoor, and the Radburn system on which it was based, was soon revealed to have problems. Huntingdonshire County Council was already expressing concerns about the high density of the housing in 1962, even as the first houses were being built. The very fact that pedestrian and public areas were separated from roads increased worries about crime: car owners could not see the car parks or garages

Underpasses were welcomed on the Oxmoor because they kept people and vehicles separate, but they became a focus for vandalism. (The authors)

from their homes and were concerned about vandalism, while the footpaths felt isolated, badly lit and dangerous. Moreover the lack of natural surveillance in the public areas, especially the greens, increased the problems of fly tipping, graffiti and petty vandalism. Those living on the estate found it difficult to integrate, particularly when local people referred to them as 'the overspill', despite the fact that from February 1962, it was decreed that the overspill development was to be referred to only as 'the Oxmoor Estate'. By 1974, the word 'estate' was formally dropped from the name.

Almost exactly a year after W. and C. French Construction Ltd completed work on the Oxmoor, in October 1970, a report in a national newspaper *The People* caused outrage among local residents. Local pastor David Coombs claimed that two thirds of those on the Oxmoor were living in poverty, that marital problems were widespread and that there was an increased crime rate. 'Oxmoor has become a dirty word as far as most traders in the town are concerned. No trader likes giving credit to anyone who says that they are from the Oxmoor. Many just refuse point blank... For some of these people it's a never ending day to day circle of scraping, borrowing, paying back and borrowing again just to keep their heads above water.'

At first many houses on the new estate stood empty, but they could not be used to house local people waiting for accommodation because they were reserved for those moving from London. This understandably caused resentment. Later, however, nobody wanted to move into them and 257 houses stood unoccupied by 1968. Eventually the families of army personnel stationed at Waterbeach moved in, and there were plans to let more houses to the USAF. This led to locals complaining that they were being priced out of local housing by US servicemen. Bad feeling towards the Americans continued, and gangs of youths roamed around terrorising Americans who lived on the Oxmoor. Rocks, broken bottles and sticks were thrown at their houses. English and American youths were often seen fighting. The Americans were not the only ones to suffer in this way. Asian families living on the estate, some of whom had been expelled from Uganda in 1972, also feared racial attack. One family living in Norfolk Road frequently had their windows smashed by bricks, endured racist chanting and had lighted fireworks pushed through the letterbox. Gangs of youths were not the only problem: packs of stray dogs roaming around caused schoolchildren to be kept in a breaktimes.

Water shortages in Huntingdon, which caused the supply tanks at the County Hospital to run dry and the level in the Hinchingbrooke water tower to fall below danger level, were blamed on increased consumption by the new factories. Established local factories were also unhappy about new companies 'poaching' their workforce. Silent Channel's Director complained 'To allow new factories to be built, without ensuring adequate labour is available to run them, is an intolerable burden on those industries already established here.'

The water tower built in St Peters Road in 1963 to ease water shortages in Huntingdon. (The authors)

In 1977 the Oxmoor estate again hit the headlines, this time for much more tragic reasons. Despite complaints from residents aircraft from nearby RAF Wyton flew regularly overhead. On 3 May 1977 a Canberra returning from a two-hour reconnaissance flight over Scotland plummeted into a row of houses in Norfolk Road, killing three young children and both crew members. Flight Lieutenant John Armitage and Flight Lieutenant Lawrence Davies tried desperately to avoid the built up area. Local resident Keith Sisman was quoted in the *Daily Express*: 'the pilot was obviously trying to get away from the houses. He must have known he was finished, but he tried to save the school and the estate'. The Canberra missed Sapley Park School where 245 children were about to go home for lunch, but its wing hit a row of houses in Norfolk Road, and blazing fuel spilled out in a ball of fire. Four-year-old Tracey Middleton and her two-year-old sister Kelly died, along with four-month-old Adrian Thompson. Six others were injured and seven houses were completely gutted. Mr Evans from Sycamore Drive said 'it was absolutely terrifying. It looked as if a giant bomb had hit the whole place. There were women crying in the street.'

The devastation in Norfolk Road following the Canberra crash on 3 May 1977. (Hunts Post)

Throughout the 1970s and 1980s the reputation of the Oxmoor did not improve, despite the fact that by 1988 a third of Huntingdon's population was living there. A report for the Children's Society, published in their magazine *The Gateway* in 1988, branded the Oxmoor 'the most deprived housing area in Cambridgeshire'. The report said that the estate was still isolated after all these years. Research showed that the Oxmoor had double the county average of single-parent families, four times the number of juvenile offenders, and three times the amount of crime compared with the rest of Huntingdon, and that it had the second highest unemployment figure in the county. This report led to serious attempts at improvement. In 1990 the Department of the Environment prom-

Inspecting the damage caused in May 1977. (Hunts Post)

The new Trinity Church, dedicated in 1968. (The authors)

ised £3 million for an Estate Action Programme, part of £190 million promised by the government. A four-stage improvement programme was begun in 1994 to create cul-de-sacs to stop easy escape by wrongdoers, provide more parking space and improve street lighting. In 1995 a former hairdressers shop in Sapley Square was transformed into the Moor Community Centre, a meeting place and advice centre. This was followed by the creation of an Oxmoor Community Action Group, which carried out a health improvement survey. As a result of health concerns the Acorn Community Health Centre was opened in 12 March 2001, partly funded from £14.5 million Single Regeneration Budget funding. This was only one of many projects aimed to improve life on the Oxmoor. The Oxmoor Opportunities Partnership combined 37 different groups working to improve conditions.

Drugs remain a major worry for many residents and discarded needles threaten the health of local children, but in 2001 the East of England Development agency promised £1.5 million to improve education and skills and to cut drug use. In May 2001 arrests were made when a mob converged on the house of alleged drug dealers. In 1998 Home Office minister Alun Michael visited the Oxmoor to see for himself how the different agencies and the police were tackling crime. Sapley Square, which was once a symbol of the decline of the estate, has been revitalised and a police drop-in centre has been set up. Moor Play, launched in September 2002, welcomes families with children to meet, play and socialise. The Oxmoor Action Plan of 2002 includes proposals for safer routes through the estate, improved play areas and recreational facilities and a better mix of housing types.

Moor Play. (Cambridgeshire Library Service)

CHAPTER 10

'Constipation Street': Traffic in Huntingdon

THE NEED for a bypass and a ring road for Huntingdon was officially recognised in the first Town Plan of 1951. Huntingdon's High Street lay on the Great North Road (the old A14) which ran northwards along Ermine Street, meeting the A1 at Alconbury Hill. Cross-country traffic ran along the A604, which connected the Midlands to Cambridge and beyond. Local, county and through traffic was being funnelled through the centre of Huntingdon. In 1947 a survey had been done of all the traffic passing through, which discovered that 4,397

Ermine Street before the advent of the motor car. (Norris Museum: PH/HUNTN/100)

The 'World's largest lorry' passes through the centre of Huntingdon in the 1930s. (County Record Office Huntingdon: WH9/31)

motor vehicles and 2,917 cyclists used the High Street in a 12-hour period. More importantly, perhaps, the survey also ascertained that 70 percent of this traffic was through traffic, which could easily be bypassed around the town. By 1959 this figure had risen to 11,443 vehicles passing along the High Street.

Despite the fact that something quite clearly needed to be done, it would be years before either a bypass or a ring road was completed. In the meantime, increased traffic was making Huntingdon High Street 'the most unpleasant, the most uncomfortable shopping centre in Huntingdonshire', full of 'heavy, noisy, fuming, hooting, splashing, smelly traffic. Traffic which seems unending'. As Huntingdon's population grew through the 1960s, things only got worse. In 1963 the Chief Constable, Mr T.C. Williams, dubbed the High Street 'constipation street' as the word 'congestion' was not strong enough. The footpath was so narrow that two prams could not pass one another without the risk of serious injury, and people

A traffic jam in the High Street, 1963. (County Record Office Huntingdon: 1096/25)

Narrow pavements along the High Street in 1963. (County Record Office Huntingdon: 1096/150)

Tricky winter driving conditions during the 1960s. (County Record Office Huntingdon: DC 251)

found it almost impossible to cross from one side to another. Between 1 December 1962 and 30 November 1963 there were 77 accidents along the High Street, 49 of which involved through traffic.

In January the following year a petition was started asking for a bypass: 'We, being loyal citizens of Her Majesty, are deeply concerned at the danger to the lives of our citizens and to the life of our county town of Huntingdon caused by the trunk road which is also our High Street. We ask Her Majesty's government to treat the provision of a bypass for Huntingdon as a matter of extreme urgency.' One thousand people signed the petition in

The disused railway bridge would become the route of the Huntingdon bypass. (County Record Office Huntingdon: WH2/6)

the first week. Soon it had some 6,000 names and a demonstration was organised for the 14 March to deliver it first to David Renton, the local MP, and then personally to the Minister. Unfortunately heavy rain spoiled the event and only 45 protesters took part.

The planned bypass would swing to the west of Huntingdon and Godmanchester, while the ring road would take the local and county traffic, enabling 'the central part of the town to fulfil its functions unhampered by a constant stream of trunk road traffic, such as now fills its only thoroughfare'. Although survey and design work for the proposed bypass began in April 1968, the bypass was still many years away, due to arguments over its route. For a while, during the early 1970s, there was even a plan to tunnel under Huntingdon rather than build a bypass around it, thereby keeping the view across Portholme. Unfortunately the Government decided against the tunnel, as it would cost about £1 million more to build than a conventional bypass.

Buildings on the approach to the bridge, demolished during the construction of the ring road. (County Record Office Huntingdon: 1096/200)

The ring road

Work on the ring road began much earlier, and was completed in stages. The section between Walden Road and Mill Common was first, followed by the section through to the Bridge Hotel. As early as 1965 a one-way system was proposed by a former resident and civil, highways and traffic engineer, Mr McDowell, but the Council argued against it before the completion of the ring road. However, in June 1969 one-way traffic was introduced along the High Street during the laying of a gas main. This proved so successful that the system was retained. Speeding along the High Street became a problem, but at least it was easier to cross.

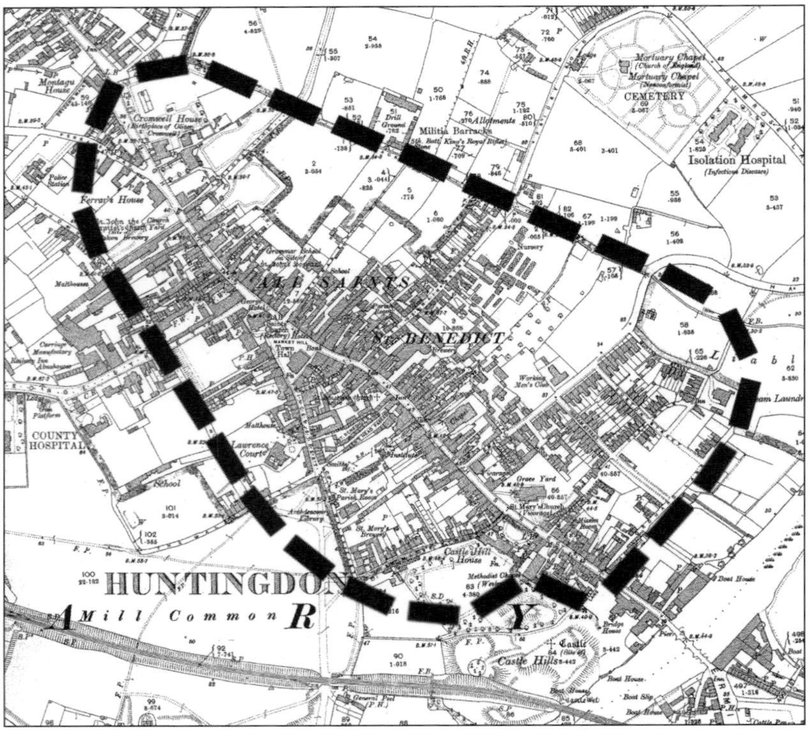

The route of the ring road, superimposed on to the 1900 Ordnance Survey map of Huntingdon.

The long-awaited ring road finally opened in June 1970, although the St John's Street section was not finished until September 1972. A one-way system was adopted to avoid large scale demolition of property. The day had been eagerly awaited by all. In May the *Hunts Post* reported that 'by the end of this month, the County Council hopes, traffic congestion in

Huntingdon High Street with its attendant annoyance and frustration to shoppers, local motorists and long distance drivers will be a thing of the past'. In the event, the opening of the ring road was not quite the success all had hoped. By 2 July, Councillor R.J. Lomax was calling the ring road the 'biggest blunder' Huntingdon had ever seen. There was no speed limit and the ring road became a race-track: traffic was travelling round at speeds of up to 60mph and pedestrians took their lives in their hands trying to cross. There were no pedestrian crossings, and urgent demands were made for a footbridge near Brookside, where it was taking up to 10 minutes to cross.

It also had the effect of cutting off the centre from the rest of the town, killing the town centre. Electoral registers from the mid-1970s show that fewer than 200 people lived within the ring road: remember that this was the same area which housed more than 2,000 people for most of Huntingdon's history. Huntingdon's historic centre was dead when people went home from work. The completion of the ring road also took vehicles out of the High Street, but only at the cost of congestion on the ring road itself, a problem which has worsened over the years. The lack of a roundabout at the junction of Hartford Road and Riverside Road made it difficult for traffic coming from out of town to merge. There were no traffic lights around the ring road, but by 1976 it was so congested that it sometimes took more than half an hour to move along one stretch. Two traffic wardens were out most evenings, directing the flow of traffic at junctions. Cars trying to get on to the ring road at St Germain Street and Hartford Road would never be let in without help from the wardens. Eventually a set of traffic lights was installed at the end of Hartford Road.

By 1986 local councillor Bill Biram said that the ring road had reached 'saturation point', and the proposed developments in the town would only exacerbate the problem. The County Council promised that there would be no more sets of traffic lights, and instead plans for a northern bypass (first proposed in 1989) were approved. Work began on the northern bypass in March 1987 and was completed early, in June 1988. The 5.6km (3.5 mile) stretch linking Hartford to the Spittals roundabout, built in 1980, cost £5.2 million.

By 1995 measures had to be taken to reduce the number of accidents on the ring road. Four new sets of traffic lights were installed to prevent merging accidents, and two continuous lanes of traffic were created to cut down on lane changes. By 2003, 10 sets of traffic lights were in operation around the ring road, causing major hold ups at peak times. A traffic monitoring report made in 2000 discovered that an astonishing 73,400 vehicles entered and left Huntingdon every day between 7.00am and 7.00pm.

The bypass at last

Twenty years after the need for a bypass had first been recognised the Government inquiry opened, and seven months later, in June 1972, the Secretary of State for the

The new bridge across the River Ouse under construction. (Hunts Post)

Environment finally gave the go ahead for the north-south bypass route. The local MP David Renton had suggested an east-west route, leading from Godmanchester to join the A1 just south of Brampton (the same route as that proposed in a report of 2001 when the bypass was unable to cope with the volume of traffic using it). Mr Renton's fears that eventually an east-west bypass would have to be built as well as the north-south one were rejected. Instead it was decided to construct a dual lane flyover across Huntingdon, without thought that it would be impossible to widen

Aerial photograph showing the bypass under construction in May 1974. (Hunts Post)

Richard Dorling, County Surveyor, opens the bypass on 30 September 1975. (Hunts Post)

in the future, and costly to maintain. The sheer complexity of the proposed flyover led to more delays, and contracts to build the bypass took almost a year to negotiate. The 10.5km (6.5 mile) long bypass was finally opened on 30 September 1975 by Richard Dorling, County Surveyor, nearly a quarter of a century after the need for it was first made apparent. After only 13 years in use the bypass needed a £4 million reconstruction. Its condition had deteriorated badly, even though only 28,000 vehicles a day were using it. This figure would more than double with the opening of the A1/M1 link road in 1993. By 2000, an average of 69,000 vehicles were using the flyover each day between 6am and 10pm.

The modern bypass and the mediaeval stone bridge. (The authors)

CHAPTER 11

'Building for the future': Hinchingbrooke and other recent developments

HINCHINGBROOKE had long been the centre of Huntingdon affairs, but after the Montagu family moved out during the war the house fell into disrepair and it was sold to the County Council in 1962. It was planned to convert the house into a school. The following year the County Council bought most of the remaining estate. Immediately plans were made to use the site for a new hospital and county council headquarters, as well as the new school. A new fire station, replacing the old building in Princes Street, opened in Hartford Road in November 1964, but almost all the other developments in Huntingdon at this time were planned for the Hinchingbrooke site. In preparation for the new developments, in November 1967 work began on the construction of an underpass and the bypassing of Nun's Bridge, a notorious accident blackspot.

Work began almost immediately on the conversion of the house, although it soon became clear that the cost would be far in excess of the original estimate of £57,000, mainly due to the discovery of dry rot. There were calls for the whole project to be abandoned, but work went ahead on what would become the new upper school of Huntingdon Grammar. The school sixth form would occupy the house, while the middle school pupils moved into purpose-built accommodation on the site of the former kitchen garden. By the time work had been completed Huntingdon County Council

Aerial view of Hinchingbrooke House, taken during the 1960s. (County Record Office Huntingdon: accession 4231A)

had taken the decision to go comprehensive, and the new school was officially opened by Mr Victor Montagu (formerly 10th Earl of Sandwich) on 18 September 1970 as a comprehensive, named Hinchingbrooke School, rather than as a grammar school. By 1987 plans were being made to move the entire school on to one site. The lower school, on the opposite side of Brampton Road, had opened in 1939 and was in a very poor state. The design and technology room was described as being like a Nissen hut. Building work began on the upper school site in January 1991. The following April a gym, a science block, a performing arts centre and 21 new classrooms were all complete. The former grammar school buildings were closed and the school was once more united on a single site. After standing empty for a year, the old school building was targeted by arsonists, and was devastated by fire. The site was subsequently developed for housing.

Hinchingbrooke School. (The authors)

The second major project planned for Hinchingbrooke was the building of a new hospital, but, as usual, the process was an extremely slow one. In fact a new police headquarters was proposed, planned, built and opened as the Mid Anglia Constabulary HQ by Prince Charles in October 1973 before work even began on the desperately needed new hospital. Work on the first phase of the new hospital, the geriatric department, finally began in 1974, and the 112-bed unit was complete by February 1976. Petersfield, the former workhouse, which had been used as a geriatric hospital, became a day centre for the physically handicapped.

Completion of the first phase of building did not mean the end of the delays, however. The poor economic climate led to threats to abandon the project completely, and it was not until 1978 that the Regional Health Authority finally gave the go ahead for the construction of the hospital. Work began in July 1979, and by January 1983 the site was handed over ready to be fitted out. More than

Cambridgeshire Constabulary headquarters at Hinchingbrooke. (The authors)

75,000 pieces of equipment, costing £3 million, had been ordered for the new building – £140,000 worth of instruments for the operating theatre alone. There were 213 beds, and accommodation for 160 staff. The total cost was £15 million.

In July the outpatients, biochemistry and pharmacy departments were transferred from the old County Hospital, and on Monday 5 September the obstetrics and maternity department opened. It was one of the most modern in the NHS, and included a special care baby unit: but it was all an anticlimax, as no babies arrived. Flowers to be presented to the first new mother had to be put on ice. It was not until the early hours of Thursday that Hinchingbrooke's first baby, Rachael, weighing 6lb 12oz, was born to Karen and Richard Newman from St Ives.

The final transfer of all services from the County Hospital was complete by the

Huntingdon County Hospital. Built in 1853, it was not able to cope with the demands of the 1970s. (Huntingdon Library)

Hinchingbrooke Hospital. (The authors)

end of October 1983. Social services, ambulance control (although the ambulance station at Hinchingbrooke had opened on 13 November 1980) and the psychiatry unit remained at Petersfield, but the plan was to sell off the site as soon as possible, as much of it was already derelict. Huntingdon Health Authority wanted to refurbish the old County Hospital for use as its HQ, but this scheme was blocked by the Regional Health Authority as being too grandiose. Huntingdon Health Authority HQ remained at Primrose Lane, and the County Hospital was sold off for £200,000. It was subsequently restored to its former splendour and converted into sheltered accommodation, the first new residents moving in by January 1987. Hinchingbrooke Hospital was officially opened a year after completion by Princess Alice, Duchess of Gloucester.

The people of Huntingdon were proud of their new hospital, and when the Hinchingbrooke MacMillan Cancer Care Appeal was launched in May 1995, they responded magnificently. The people of Huntingdonshire District raised £900,000 in less than two years (including £250,000 donated by the Freeman's Charity) and the new Woodlands Centre was opened in January 1998 by the Prince of Wales.

By 2000 health services in Huntingdon were again at full stretch, despite the fact that the hospital now had over 300 beds. In 2001 a £16-million expansion scheme for a new Ambulatory Care and Diagnostic centre, to be opened in 2005, was announced.

While the hospital was being constructed another prestigious project was completed at Hinchingbrooke. In May 1983 William Whitelaw, the Home Secretary, opened the new police forensic laboratory. The forensic lab had been transferred from Nottingham the November before, and served 10 constabularies. In 1988 it became one of the first centres to carry out DNA profiling.

The idea of a creating a country park at Hinchingbrooke had been proposed as far back as 1970, but it could not go ahead until gravel extraction had been completed, and the final go ahead for the park was not given until December 1985. Hinchingbrooke Country Park was the first such park in Cambridgeshire. A joint project between Cambridgeshire County Council, Huntingdonshire District Council and the Countryside Commission, it was made up of 150 acres of woodland, meadows and riverbank. There were three lakes, two of which had been created by gravel extraction, while the other had been the original boating lake of the Montagu family. The culmination of almost 20 years planning, the park was opened by the actor Nigel Hawthorne on 23 April 1989. Unfortunately, as so often in the history of Huntingdon, the event was marred by torrential rain! Further developments at the park included the construction of an Iron-Age farm and the building of a new countryside centre, which was opened by John Major, one of his last acts as Huntingdon MP, in February 2001.

Hinchingbrooke Country Park, with the new Countryside Centre on the right. (The authors)

In the late 1980s and into the 1990s, as Huntingdon continued to expand, further developments were made on the former Hinchingbrooke estate, which

The Iron Age farm at Hinchingbrooke Country Park. (The authors)

St Benedict's Court as it appeared in 1963. (County Record Office Huntingdon: 1096/12)

The new St Benedict's Court under construction. (Hunts Post)

headquarters, which was handling six times the number of books processed in 1947. The new building at Huntingdon was finally opened on 24 September 1971, shortly after a fire at the old branch, Gazeley House, had destroyed many books and library records. The new building consisted of an adult and junior lending library on the ground floor with a reference and local history area on the first floor gallery. The new building actually offered a third less public shelving area, but there was a purpose-built stack area.

The social scene may have been poor in Huntingdon, but the Oxmoor development had given a boost to local industry. As seen in previous chapters, Huntingdon had never been an industrial town, but in the 1960s manufacturing industry really began to take off in Huntingdon. Between 1961 and 1971 more than 30 firms were established along St Peter's Road, Windover Road, Redwongs Way and Glebe Road, including Myers, Vitaulic, Stewarts and Lloyds, Lola Cars, Specialised Mouldings and Harcostar. The development along St Peter's Road was virtually complete by the early 1970s. Insulpak was later built on a site previously allocated for a primary school. The number of manufacturing jobs in Huntingdon doubled between 1963 and 1973.

The new library in Princes Street being built, 1971. (Cambridge Evening News)

Despite problems in the early 1980s – when Vitaulic was forced to go on to a four day week, Harcostar had to cut almost 25 percent of their workforce, and Silent Channel almost 50 percent of theirs – industry in Huntingdon remained relatively buoyant. Development of the Stukeley Meadows site began in 1979. It included about 50 small units for new businesses. Mission Electronics and Bright Instruments were the largest firms on this site. Bright had moved to Huntingdon in 1963, into a small factory in St Peter's Road. The company had prospered and expanded into new premises, opened in April 1985 by Kenneth Clarke, Minister for Health. Building on the Stukeley Meadows industrial area was complete by 1986–7.

St Peters Road industrial area, 1974. (Hunts Post)

During the 1980s Huntingdon was the fastest growing town in the fastest growing county in the country. Population growth exceeded 18 percent. Much of this development was due to industrial pressures being felt in Cambridge. Good transport links, which included the A14/M11 corridor, the A1 and the proposed A1/M1 link road, served to fuel this growth. A 1988 survey showed that Huntingdon was the seventh most prosperous town in the entire country. In the same year work began on the new Ermine Business Park, which attracted high profile international companies such as Nokia Telecommunications. Subsequently land owned by St John's College was developed by St Johns/Grosvenor Developments. The recession of the early 1990s did not hit Huntingdon so badly as many other areas. Having the local MP, John Major, as Prime Minister did much to raise the profile of the town; and the long awaited opening of the A1/M1 link road, in 1993, was another incentive for incoming business development. New business parks continued to spring up: Hinchingbrooke Business Park was launched in 1993–4 and Vantage Park in 1999.

The Nokia building at the entrance to the Ermine Business Park. (The authors)

Housing development continued apace too. Four developers were allocated 110 acres to build on in Stukeley Meadows, using 40 different house designs. John Major officially opened the new estate in April 1988. Stukeley Meadows School opened in September 1992. Further housing developments sprang up at Hinchingbrooke Park, Sapley Road and Hartford.

John Major, former Prime Minister, campaigning in Huntingdon in 2001. (Huntingdon Constituency Conservative Association)

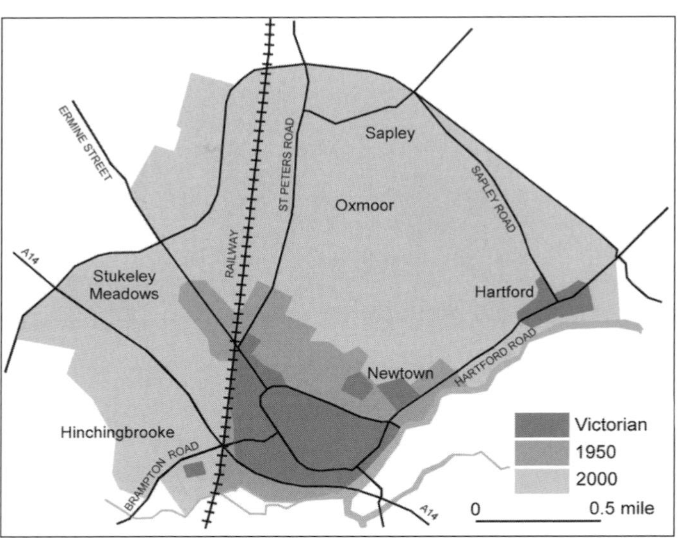

How Huntingdon has grown from the 19th century to the beginning of the 21st. (The authors)

Spring Common

The most controversial proposals for new housing were the plans to build on Spring Common. Part of Spring Common had been subject to compulsory purchase for the Oxmoor development in 1958, but the ownership of the common was a complex issue and had never really been resolved. After 1967 the common was administered by a charitable trust for the benefit of the few remaining Freemen of Huntingdon. This trust was granted permission by the Charity Commission to sell part of the common, and this is what they did. In 1989 Welland Homes paid £2.5 million for 6½ acres of Spring Common. Local people had been campaigning against the development of Spring Common for many years, and in 1986 SCANDAL (Spring Common Against New Development of Ancient Land) had been formed after planning permission was granted. The proposed development included the site of the former Petersfield Hospital, the access land to which was already owned by the Council.

The campaigners made Spring Common a national issue, partly due to the fact that it was, by now, in the Prime Minister's constituency. The cause was championed by Lord Denning who urged Huntingdon residents to 'fight with the same

Left: *Huntingdon Technical College in California Road, photographed in 1971. The college was opened in 1966.* (Hunts Post)

Right: *The demolition of Petersfield Hospital, as part of the Spring Common development.* (Nick Clifford)

stout courage as their old grammar school boy Oliver Cromwell', and tabled a question about Spring Common in the House of Lords. In March 1992, the court ruled that the Freemen should lose their exclusive rights to the common, and a new trust was set up to benefit the inhabitants of Huntingdon as a whole. An appeal against this decision by the Freemen was turned down by Lord Justice Morritt in 1993. He ruled that the sale of the land had been illegal, and that it should be bought back if the new trustees saw fit. A further appeal to the European court also failed.

The actual fate of the disputed area of Spring Common was still undecided however, and work began on a new access road in Lammas Gardens in 1996. A year later, the new trustees announced that they would not buy back the land, which could now cost up to £3.5 million, as it would not be an economic use of their funds. When planning permission was passed by single vote by Huntingdonshire District Council, this time to Barratts, the protestors tried a new avenue of attack. They claimed that Spring Common was the site of a Civil War earthwork which would need archaeological investigation before building could proceed. This failed when the county archaeologists denied that there was any archaeological evidence worth preserving. The fight to save this part of Spring Common from development finally ended in 2000 when an application to have it registered as a town green was refused by the County Council. By this time, Barratts had almost completed the development of 71 houses anyway. The remainder of Spring Common is currently managed as a public open space.

The spring on Spring Common. (The authors)

'Shopping frenzy'

Plans were made to build out of town shopping facilities for the growing population. Both Tesco and Sainsbury put in applications to build out of town stores. Huntingdon's first 'out of town' store Texas Homecare (now Dunelm) had opened in Stukeley Road in June 1984, but only because accommodation could not be found in the town centre. The District Council was still keen to develop the centre, and in

June 1986 plans were unveiled for a £12-million shopping centre for Huntingdon. Two rival developers were involved, and negotiations would take 12 years. Sainsbury's in the meantime wanted to build on a 7.6 acre site at Hartford, but after lengthy discussions planning permission was refused. Tesco, however, eventually gained permission to build on Abbots Ripton Road. Huntingdon's first superstore opened in 1992. The new store caused what *The Hunts Post* described as 'shopping frenzy'. On the opening day the car park was full and shoppers parked on a nearby roundabout and along the road. Traffic queued along the bypass and down St Peter's Road. The store's popularity continued and it soon became one of the five busiest Tesco stores in the country.

Left: *The new Tesco superstore on Abbots Ripton Road, under construction. The store was opened by Norma Major in August 1992.* (Nick Clifford)

Right: *Towerfields.* (The authors)

The building of Tesco was the catalyst for further development on what became known as the Towerfields site. Further out of town stores were built and an application for a leisure complex on the former sports pitches was submitted. A rival bid for development in St Peter's Road was rejected due to the detrimental effect it would have on the school. In July 2000 a multi-screen cinema, Cineworld, opened at Towerfields with *Mission Impossible 2*, and with it came fast food outlets, a restaurant and leisure complex. Finally, the young people of Huntingdon had something to entertain them.

In the meantime, negotiations for a town centre development were still dragging on. Everyone recognised that the town centre was suffering from out of town competition. In September 1994 the Huntingdonshire District Council Planning Committee stated 'we are conscious, that, following the opening of the out of town Tesco, the existing supermarkets in the town have suffered a trading impact… the town requires a significant qualitative improvement of retail provision in order to 'claw back' substantial levels of trade currently leaking to competing facilities. In particular, the need to attract the car borne food shopper through the provision of a modern large foodstore is in our view essential.' Councillor Mike Robertson put it more succinctly: 'we have a dead centre in Huntingdon which needs to be regenerated'.

It would be another three years before planning permission was finally granted for the building of a Sainsbury's store, seven other shops, a car park for 410 cars

Left: *Murketts Garage on the ring road, photographed in May 1983. The garage was demolished for the St Germain's Walk development.* (County Record Office Huntingdon: accession 3312)

Right: *St Germain Street in 1963.* (County Record Office Huntingdon: 1096/141)

and a petrol station on the site of the former Ruston's premises and Murkett's garage. Eighteen months later St Germain Street was closed, a new access road opened, and work began on the Sainsburys store. Chequers Court, built 40 years before, was showing its age and was included in the redevelopment. When a new Post Office opened in St Germain's Walk Huntingdon had a Post Office with its own premises for the first time since the one in Chequers Court had been closed. Plans to develop an Aldi supermarket on the former Brookside school site, however, came to nothing.

Overall the new developments, despite causing further congestion on the Huntingdon ring road, did fulfil expectations, and Huntingdon's town centre has begun to attract new shops and businesses.

Chequers Court in 2004. (The authors)

celebrate the quatercentenary of Cromwell's birth, which included a street market, as well as lectures by well-known figures, displays and exhibitions spanning more than six months, were so successful that a similar Pepys weekend was held in 2003. The mediaeval celebrations planned to commemorate the granting of Huntingdon's first charter in 1205 suggest that these historical events will be a regular feature of the modern day town. Huntingdon has become the thriving modern town that generations of councils have strived for, but one that is not afraid to celebrate its past.

Index